Make Some Noise

music PRO guides
guides

Make Some Noise

Become the Ultimate DJ

Scott Binder

Hal Leonard Books
AN IMPRINT OF HAL LEONARD CORPORATION

Published in 2014 by Hal Leonard Books
An Imprint of Hal Leonard Corporation
7777 West Bluemound Road
Milwaukee, WI 53213

Trade Book Division Editorial Offices
33 Plymouth St., Montclair, NJ 07042

Printed in the United States of America

Book design by Adam Fulrath

Library of Congress Cataloging-in-Publication Data

Binder, Scott, author.
 Make some noise : become the ultimate DJ / Scott Binder.
    pages ; cm
1. Disc jockeys--Vocational guidance. I. Title.
 ML3795B56 2013
 781.4--dc23
                                        2013035714

ISBN 978-1-4803-5045-8

www.halleonardbooks.com

Contents

Acknowledgments

I would like to express gratitude to the many people who helped my book, *Make Some Noise,* become a reality. The process has truly been a life-changing experience, and I appreciate everyone's feedback and support. First and foremost, I would like to thank my parents for instilling in me the attitude not only that I could accomplish anything I set my mind to do but also that following my dreams was important.

I would like to thank my publisher, Hal Leonard Performing Arts Publishing Group; John Cerullo, for publishing *Make Some Noise* and believing in my vision; and Matt Cerullo, for his editing advice. I've read many of Hal Leonard's well-crafted books on audio production, so I am very proud to be part of their family. I would like to thank my great agent, Rita Rosenkranz, for her professionalism and support and for being an amazing guide in my writing career. A thank-you also goes to Brandon LaFave for dropping everything to read over my book before I sent out the proposal. I would like to thank the DJs featured in my book as well as their managers for always getting back to me so quickly. This book would not have the same impact without them.

A special thanks to the video crew: Simeon, Geyer (camera and directing), Daniel Feigl (camera and audio), and Luca Leinemann (editing). And last but certainly not least, I would like to thank the most talented motion graphic artist that I know, Nathan Heal, for creating the intro for the DVD. Your work is truly among the best in the world, and I am grateful you created such a cool intro for the video.

Special thanks to two record labels that I have a ton of respect for, Formatik Records and Made Fresh Daily, for letting me feature their music in the video.

Music credits for the video:

1. Formatik Records: Pleasurekraft & Format:B, "Coltrane" feat. Chris The Voice
2. Made Fresh Daily: Swoose, "Rushin" (JMX Bossin' Remix)
3. Scott Binder & Roland Clark, "I Got What You Want"
4. Scott Binder & Edwin Jesus, "Let's Get This Thing Started"
5. Scott Binder feat. Blue MC, "Freedom" (The Banger Bros Remix)
6. Scott Binder feat. Melakai, "Good Time Tonight" (Hoxton Whores Remix)

I would also like to thank the audio companies below, who helped make the video for *Make Some Noise* possible. I have the most respect for you, and I'm grateful you were part of this project.

Make Some Noise

Introduction

"If I could say what I had to say in words, I would have never become a producer/DJ. When words leave off, music begins."
—Yasmin le Bon

What Is DJ'ing?

A DJ can be called many things, and sometimes people lump the titles DJ and music producer all into one meaning. But a DJ is first and foremost an entertainer who selects and blends music into one continuous mix to play for an audience. Although the type of music one plays is an integral part of DJ'ing, there is more to the craft than simply selecting a desirable song and pressing the Play button. Being a DJ is about performance, crowd interaction, and the art and craft of seamlessly mixing two songs together to create one continuous track. When DJs are performing, it's important that they read the crowd's reaction to gauge whether the audience is enjoying the music as much as they are. As a DJ, when you play tracks that you enjoy, you naturally think that the audience will enjoy them as much as you do. But sometimes that is not the case, and even if the audience enjoys a certain track, sometimes the placement of it might be off, thereby creating an undesirable effect, so paying attention to the reaction of the people out on the dance floor is critical. A great DJ performance is one where the crowd is dancing so much that their clothes are drenched in sweat when it's time to go home. If people have a great time, your show is a success. Ultimately, we DJ because we love how it feels, but its purpose is to entertain and provide the crowd with a release. When patrons come to a show, it's because they are looking for a place to relieve stress and have fun. If DJs are doing what they are supposed to, they are serving as a conduit for this exact experience.

In 1909, the world was introduced to its first DJ—a sixteen-year-old college student in San Jose, California, by the name of Ray Newby. A lot has changed since the late Newby played records on the airwaves from the college radio station at Herrold College of Engineering and Wireless in San Jose. Over the years, especially in the last ten to fifteen, the art and craft of DJ'ing has changed dramatically. Unless we fill our parents in on what's going on, most of them have no clue about what a DJ really is. Isn't it someone on the radio who introduces music and presses Play on the record player? Times have changed. Whether a DJ is a club jock or a radio personality, the fundamental elements of being considered a DJ are playing, selecting, and mixing music. Older generations simply believe that a DJ is someone who puts a record on, plays it to the end, picks the record up off the player and puts it on the same turntable, and presses Play once again.

Many people in the current generation believe a DJ should be mixing on vinyl, and if they aren't, they aren't a "real" DJ. I started DJ'ing at the tail end of the vinyl era, so I've seen the culture shift from records to CDs and now to software. Many of my fellow DJ friends are complaining about laptop DJ'ing, and my advice to you on this particular subject is that when the generation after you introduces yet another technological advancement in DJ'ing, embrace it. If you do, the transition from what you are comfortable with to what is next will be much smoother.

With the recent developments in technology, DJ'ing has turned its attention to the computer generation. This has opened up a world of possibilities and is changing the culture right before our eyes. Of course, there are a lot of traditionalists who believe that the art form of DJ'ing is being lost in the technology, but I disagree. It's simply providing yet another platform for the craft to evolve and expand. True, mixing records is a craft that takes much longer to perfect than mixing on a computer-based system, but I believe that the computer system provides opportunities for DJs to incorporate instruments, drum machines, synthesizers, and any other controller one sees fit. This opens a world to DJs truly creating a live show. Even if a DJ has no intention of including live elements or controllers into their sets, I have no problem with the computer-based mixing systems. Sure, one can incorporate live instrumentation on the traditional setups. I am one of those who do that. But technology makes this possibility even easier. After all, there is much more to DJ'ing than beatmatching and mixing. Does this mean I personally would DJ on a computer-based program without playing an instrument? No, but I think that if we resist change we are closing ourselves off to what lies on the other side as we sift through the ever-changing landscape of the music world.

To become an ultimate DJ, one must master all levels of DJ'ing. And in my opinion, DJ'ing consists of these elements: mixing and beatmatching, programming amazing sets, incorporating live instrumentation, and crowd interaction. If you master these elements, you will separate yourself from 99 percent of the DJs out there. Sometimes good DJs excel at mixing but completely lose sight of their crowd. Other DJs are great at connecting with people on the dance floor but lack proficiency at mixing or programming their sets. It doesn't mean a DJ is necessarily bad if he or she doesn't master all levels of DJ'ing. A good DJ is pretty good at most of the facets of DJ'ing but isn't a master of any of them. Is it a bad thing to be a good DJ? Not at all, but being great means mastering as many levels of the craft as possible. Modern DJs are at their best when they are turning their shows into true live performance, and mastering all of the levels illustrated in this book will help you do that.

My Story

On a hot summer afternoon when I was twelve years old, I remember playing along to Mötley Crüe's "Girls, Girls, Girls" on my brother's shiny maroon Tama drum set in his bedroom in our basement. I've always been someone who is attracted to dynamic experiences, and when I was pounding the drumsticks in time to Mötley Crüe, I daydreamed about being onstage performing in front of thousands of screaming fans. At that time Mötley Crüe was my favorite rock 'n' roll band, and Tommy Lee was my favorite drummer. It was at that moment I remember thinking that when I grew up I wanted to be a rock 'n' roll drummer and a major league baseball player. I had already had the dream of becoming a professional baseball player, and now I was inspired to follow in the footsteps of Tommy Lee. The memory is as vivid as though it had happened today. A few years later, I decided to put my music aspirations on hold to become a major league baseball player. I signed a professional contract in January of 1999 and it looked as though I had a promising career, but it was cut short that spring when I was released in large part because of my drug and alcohol addictions.

Around this time, I was an avid club goer in the electronic dance music (EDM) scene and I fell in love with dance music. I distinctly remember going to an after-hours club called Habanas in Seattle during the early part of the morning. While watching the DJ spin, I thought to myself, "One day I want travel the world as a DJ and producer." The seeds of my music aspirations had been reawakened, but first I had to put my life back together. About six months later, my life came crashing down. I had hit bottom, and I checked myself into an inpatient drug rehab center.

At this time I officially lost my dream of becoming a major league baseball player, but more importantly, I had almost lost my life because of my drug and alcohol addictions and reckless actions. But all things considered, I was fortunate for two reasons: I was alive and had learned a life lesson at a young age. At twenty-three, I saw firsthand how addictions destroy lives. I knew that if I was able to stay sober, I still had my whole life ahead of me and I could still achieve my dreams. And for those who are wondering—no, it doesn't matter what age you choose to embark on your path as a DJ. I've seen people start at ten, and I've seen others begin their journey at forty or older. There are no rules and everything is achievable if you want it badly enough and are willing to put in the work. The only thing to consider is that depending on how big your vision and goals are for DJ'ing, some of them will happen relatively quickly, while others may take longer to come to fruition. As the phrase goes, "Rome wasn't built in a day." With that being said, some people certainly experience big success faster than others, so it really comes down to what you allow to happen. Success is different for each person, so define it based on what you want it to be, not what others think it is.

While I was in rehab, the urge to get back into music grew stronger by the day. Shortly after being successfully discharged from the inpatient treatment, a mentor of mine introduced the African drum called the *djembe* to me, and I fell in love. I had officially found my new drug of choice. But this time, the choice was a healthy one. After I completed treatment, I decided to go back to school to study music, percussion, and sound production. My music journey was officially underway.

Fast-forward ten years, and I am now grateful to say that I am living a dream that is similar to the one I envisioned during my darkest days. Today, along with my friend Naite Heal, I am the cocreator of the popular EDM project called the Banger Bros. Recently, I launched my solo project, and I am getting thumbs-up reactions from house music legends Todd Terry, Fatboy Slim, DJ Dan, and Roland Clark, to name just a few. I also own the rapidly growing record label Golden Needle Records.

Naite and I met through my younger sister several years ago in the spring of 2008, and upon meeting we instantly decided to create a music partnership. After being involved in many projects with other people—ranging from working with rock, downtempo, and electronica bands to performing with a Grammy Award–winning percussionist in a group called the Drum Cafe—I finally found a partner who had the same vision of wanting to mix live instruments with high-energy dance music. In just four years of collaboration and hard work, we are now a well-known and ever-expanding group.

Our songs are played on many of the dance radio stations around the world, and so far, we've had a song on the *Billboard* Dance/Electronic Charts, called "I See Fire," featuring the vocalist Jacinta. The second song, "I Believe," featuring Julie Thompson, climbed all the way to No. 2 in the Music Week Top 100 in the UK. Our song "Beep Beep Boom," featuring Melakai, reached No. 3 on the Music Week Top 100, UK, and was also featured on MTV's *Real World*. Our music has been in countless dance charts around the world, and we've been featured in many of the dance music magazines, including *Mixmag*, *DJ Mag*, *M8*, and more. As of last winter, we signed a music publishing deal with Warner Music, and we are currently working on a collaboration with two of the members from Limp Bizkit. We are proud of our accomplishments so far and are looking forward to more. On top of all of it, I am able to travel around the world to perform live shows in places such as New York City, London, San Francisco, Toronto, Rome, Miami, Seattle, Mexico, Chisinau, Moldova, Berlin, and many more. Once I made up my mind about wanting to pursue music, I gave it everything I had. The point here is that if you turn your focus to your dreams, you can make it happen. What an amazing life music can create!

Every dream is a journey and a process. First is the incubation stage, in which you have the dream or an idea swimming around in your brain. Then you must take action and see it through. Every dream takes dedication, time, effort, and work, and I firmly believe that the only reason people sometimes don't fulfill their goals is because they give up too soon. Many times people quit right before they could have achieved major success. It's a shame, but true. As long as you stick to your dreams, they can happen for you. Or sometimes a goal or dream might not happen because there is something better in store for you. I for one am truly grateful that my dream of becoming a major league baseball player didn't happen, or the vision for having a downtempo electronic outfit changed into instead doing what I'm doing now. After attending sound-production school, I moved back to Seattle and started a live electronica trio, but we never got the project off the ground. Around that time I was a big fan of groups like Massive Attack and Everything But The Girl, so I wanted to create something similar but with my own twist. Thankfully, that vision moved toward a direction I was more aligned with, and it's what I am doing now. As a result, I am having more fun doing what I'm doing, so it's good that those particular dreams did not happen. There was simply something better for me.

At first, your dream will feel fresh and exciting, and in my experience, there seems to be a beginner's luck factor when embarking on the journey. Perhaps the world tends to bring us some good fortune quickly as a way of saying, Yes, you are on the right path—keep going! After the initial phase, things might get challenging, but this doesn't have to be all negative. It's simply the world giving you feedback about what you need to improve on. There will be struggles and you might come up against some walls, but you will find nuggets of success to go along with many valuable lessons. What's most important when you do come across challenges is the state of your attitude. If you focus only on what's not working and stay in the problem, then you will feel down longer. But if you look at the struggles directly, deal with what needs to be dealt with, and trust that everything is working out exactly as it's supposed to, then you'll move through the tough spots more quickly.

I think most people get caught up in wanting everything to happen "right now," and if it doesn't, they think they have failed. I too have fallen into the trap of wanting things to happen very quickly. At each step of the way, I said to myself, "If only I had X, then I would be happy." Well, sure enough, at each step of the way many of my wishes have been granted. Once I arrived at that X place, I thought it would solve everything, but I found myself wanting more. It's natural for us to think that way, and it's a good trait to have because it drives us to achieve more. But it can also be a trap if you never stop to appreciate what you've accomplished up to that point. The key here is to be grateful for everything that we have right now in this very moment. The journey truly is the most fulfilling part of our dreams. If you can really grab that concept, your life will be a lot more fun. It's all about the journey, not the destination.

How to Use This Book

The best way to use this book is to first read it in its entirety from cover to cover. Once you have done that, I recommend rereading the text, this time having a pen, pad or computer handy in case you want to take notes. If you already have your DJ equipment, feel free to read the book near your system, so you can practice techniques right away. But if you have a different reading style, you are welcome to use whatever suits you best. It is typical to not retain all the information after reading something just once. In fact, we retain more information by writing down what we learned and by practicing it. Like perfecting the craft of DJ'ing, the more you read this book and take notes, the more it'll be ingrained in the bedrock of your mind. Between the content I am teaching you and the spotlight pages from the DJs featured in the book, you have at your disposal tips of the trade from the best of the best in the entire world. Soak it in and enjoy the ride.

Part I

Getting Started

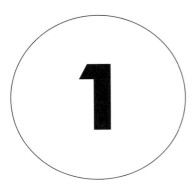

So You Want to Be a DJ?

> "When we first heard Prodigy's *Experience* album, we knew that we wanted to do this!" —Bingo Players

As you embark on your journey of becoming a DJ, it's important to discover why you want to be one and the road you wish to take to get there. It's common to not know the exact road, however, and it's likely that you will change your style many times, so have fun with any musical direction you choose. That's why it's important to ask yourself why you want to do what you're doing. The more attention and time you give to learning this art form, the more solid your vision will become. If you already know, great—but asking yourself these questions will reinforce and perhaps expand your vision. The important thing to do here is to ask yourself where you would like this journey to go. And don't worry if the answers don't come right away. If you keep asking questions and stay in action, the answers will come.

Being flexible along your journey is key. Remember earlier when I spoke about how I wanted to be a rock 'n' roll drummer when I grew up? The fact that I am not in a rock 'n' roll band does not mean that I was off in my initial inquiry at twelve years old; it simply means that I had a desire to create music. And since I was open to the medium of which I create and perform, it led me to my passion to be an EDM (electronic dance music) artist and DJ. If you are clear about your passions, the road to travel down will be revealed as long as you remain flexible and open to the process.

If you are reading this book, it's likely because something about DJ'ing inspired you and has piqued your interest to the point of considering becoming a DJ yourself. Or maybe you are already one, and you are like me in that you have a thirst for knowledge regarding anything that might take your game to the next level. There are many different reasons why people want to become a DJ. Some people simply love the idea of sharing their passion and love of music with other people. Others love discovering new music that they can introduce to their friends and fans alike. And still others love the idea of traveling the world and becoming a star. The reasons for becoming a DJ are endless.

I know some people who are frustrated with those who get involved only in order to become famous. I don' think your reasons for wanting to learn this craft matter, other than the fact that it's always good to know what your intentions are so you are clear about what you are doing. If you want to be famous, go for it! If you just want to play for your friends, throw a party! The "why" is not particularly important, so don't worry about being judged for what kind of direction you want to take. I suggested you ask yourself why you want to learn how to DJ because doing so will ultimately help you define what kind of direction you want to go in. And by the way, if you have no particular direction, that is of course totally fine, too. As you begin your journey, the only thing that matters is that you remember that life is about having fun—do that, and how it all unfolds will be exciting.

Story

When I was learning how to DJ, I didn't wait long before I tested my new skills at a club. Looking back on it, I don't regret my approach of taking action before I had perfected my skills, because my ability to get in there and just do it is part of what makes me who I am. I have a tendency to take action first and ask questions later. It is certainly one of the traits that have gotten me where I am now. If you wait until everything is perfect, you'll miss out on a mountain of opportunities. With that said, though, I definitely logged plenty of error-filled performances that cost me losing dance floors! But overall, the experiences were mostly positive and provided learning experiences that can only be achieved when you get behind the booth or onstage. They gave me that feedback I mentioned earlier that is an important element in learning how to improve. If you are willing to put yourself out there quickly, just be prepared to face some potential criticism.

Some of my fellow DJ friends tell me that they practiced in their basement for years before they felt comfortable enough to play in front of a crowd. If you do this, that's fine, too. It's a recommended approach by many, but I have never done anything this way. I firmly believe in the philosophy of pushing your limits. Taking positive risks is one of the best ways for you to go beyond what you think is possible. With that said, I recommend that you have at least a fairly strong grasp on DJ'ing before getting yourself out there. Be smart about it. I mention that some people like to practice more than others because we are all different. If you're someone who prefers to play things a bit more safely, that works, too. You will know when you are ready to play in front of others. And in my opinion, the sooner the better!

The first time I really felt like I entertained the crowd was many shows into my career. A friend of mine and I used to throw parties in San Francisco. After our events, Alex (the friend I previously mentioned) would give me feedback about what went well and where I needed improvement. Alex was not a DJ, but he loved house music and knew a good DJ performance when he heard one. Even though it was sometimes the case, I was glad that he never came out and said I stunk up the joint. Although I was frustrated and sometimes upset by certain comments of his, I knew he made good points. I always appreciated the compassion he demonstrated through this process with me. Some people will try to cut you down just because they are miserable. So if possible, avoid those people and make sure you surround yourself with those who encourage you but at the same time provide you with honest feedback that will help you grow as a DJ.

Finally, after one of our events at the Bambuddha Lounge in San Francisco, I noticed that a lot more people were dancing and having fun than usual. It felt really good to see everybody smiling and dancing during my entire set. Alex played an integral part in helping me to see that sometimes I would have to adjust the vibe of my set, depending on where I was playing. Finally! Afterward, Alex was beaming and told me that I was awesome and that it was the best show he had seen in a long time. An even bigger compliment was that Alex doesn't particularly like the kind of style that I play, but to this day, he is able to spot a good performance when he sees one. Because I live in Berlin now, Alex and I don't do regular events anymore, but he invites me to play at LovEvolution, one of the biggest EDM festivals in the United States, every year in San Francisco.

The Different Genres and Styles of Music

> "There's just something magical about DJ'ing. Being able to bring unity to an audience is the greatest feeling as a performer and a DJ." —Franko Carino (Limp Bizkit)

Today there are more subcategories and genres of music than flavors of ice cream. And that's in EDM alone! There are the obvious genres such as pop music, hip-hop, rock 'n' roll, alternative, R&B, country music, and so on. When it comes to EDM, there seems to be a new genre being created every couple of years. From house, to trance, electro, techno, tech house breaks, and minimal to dubstep, drum 'n' bass, drumstep, and glitch-hop—the list goes on. Many genres use sonic elements (that is, instrument sounds and effects) from different genres, which creates a unique sound and also further complicates things with regard to figuring out which genre should be called what. As it is, many people have difficulty correctly categorizing genres, but with lots of listening practice and keeping up with the evolution of music production, you'll be able to do it.

It is important for you to define your sound with regard to what type of music you spin as a DJ and create as a producer (if you choose that route as well). Through time, your fans and friends will come to expect a certain sound from you, so it's important to develop your own unique taste. Now this does not mean that you have to stick to only one genre. I like to vary my sets, but there is definitely a similar vibe between them. I might not always play electro or funky house, but I like things banging and funky, and people who attend my shows can expect that the vibe will be high energy, featuring tunes that straight-up bring it.

When I was starting out, I played a lot of San Francisco and Chicago house, and then I went through a stretch of switching to playing mainly big-room electro tracks. During this period, I played mostly electro and nothing else. I became stubborn with my taste in music. I'm not saying that this is the wrong way to go about it, but at some point I had to ask myself why, because I loved many styles of dance music, was I limiting my sets and sound to playing only electro? The moment I realized this, it gave me a newfound freedom, and as a result, my shows are much more fun—not only for the people dancing, but also for me because I am more flexible in what I play. I'm not saying that you should start taking people's requests . . . I certainly don't. But if you like different styles of music and it works to play them in the context of your set, go for it! I also realize that some people don't like a wide variety of music. If you are someone who plays only techno or likes only dubstep, there's nothing wrong with DJ'ing only that music. My point is that if you do enjoy a range of music, see if you can blend genres together in your sets.

Let's take a deeper look into some of the most popular genres in EDM. And in case you need a quick overview of a few genres outside of the dance music world, I'll briefly go over some of those as well. Let me warn you about something really quick. The genres in EDM are constantly changing, and the elements that define them morph into other genres to change the nature of each subgenre. For example, I was just in San Francisco for a show of mine and was talking to a couple of friends about how genres have changed. Their interpretation and understanding of what deep house is was a little dated. We were listening to what they called minimal techno. At that point I mentioned to them that what they were listening to is now considered deep house. They were surprised and didn't believe me at first, so I directed them to the deep house Top 10 Chart on Beatport, a digital download store that is geared toward DJs. "Wow," they said, "that's weird." Yes, it is interesting how genres change, and what used to be considered one thing now morphs into another. With that being said, though, the deep house they grew up on would still be considered deep house—it's just that because of the mixing of elements, each genre's scope has expanded a bit. Because we experience genres that change over time, I highly recommend that you study a few of the groundbreaking tracks in several genres. This will give you an idea of where the genres started out and how much they have or haven't evolved.

Electronic Dance Music (EDM)

Electronic dance music includes all styles of electronic music. Think of EDM as the head of the musical landscape of electronic music. Whether it's house music, techno, or dubstep, it's all considered EDM.

House Music

Many people believe that house music started in Chicago in the early 1980s, spreading out to other major cities such as London, New York, Paris, Detroit, and San Francisco. Early definitions of the genre described house music as featuring slamming 4/4 beats, rhythms, synth lines mainly consisting of drum machines, and disco samples. This style was considered to be similar to disco music, but its digital nature made the sound unique. Once house music hit Europe in the 1980s, it really took off there and emerged in many ways to be their pop music. Below are a few examples of the classic house music sound.

Chicago House

Developed in the mid to late 1980s, Chicago house is in essence proper house music, but given that many of the DJ/producers were based in Chicago, the industry paid respect to their work by creating this style name.

San Francisco House

San Francisco house, unlike Chicago house, is not necessarily a style that everyone recognizes, but I believe it needs to be. The famous record label OM Records was created in San Francisco, and even though the sound was an extension of the house music movement, the music coming out of that city via OM Records in the mid-1990s and beyond are classic and will be timeless.

Examples:
Jesse Saunders—"On & On." Considered by many to be the first house music track.
The House Master Boyz—"House Nation." One of the tracks responsible for bringing more global awareness to the genre.
Todd Terry—"Back to the Beat." Todd is a living legend in the house music world. Listen to any of his tracks to find out what proper house music is all about. Todd is a music pioneer and was one of the DJ/producers who helped define the house scene in New York City back in the 1980s.

If you listen to the above examples, they will give you a great idea of where house music came from, and you'll start to hear how things expanded into different genres. For example, after listening to these tracks just now, I heard a lot of elements from techno, tech house, deep house, and more. As you've probably figured out, house music is the ground-floor genre for all things considered to be within the house genre. deep house, soulful house, electro house, and progressive house all stem from it.

Deep House

Deep house also originated in the 1980s, but with a heavy influence in jazz, funk, and soul music. When I think of deep house, I think of saxophones, soulful vocals, and jazzy elements. If you hear a heavy jazz influence in an EDM track, it's most likely going to be deep house or funky house. Deep house is melody driven and is similar to proper house and funky house but tends to be a little more chilled out and loungy. Ever heard one of the Buddha Bar compilations? The Buddha Bar is a record label that releases chill-out music compilations, and a lot of the tracks featured on them are deep house.

> **Examples:**
> Mr. Fingers—"Can You Feel It"
> Derrick May—"Strings of Life"

Electro House

Another subgenre of house music, electro, has evolved over time, and different countries around the world have varied takes on what exactly makes up electro. The style features a heavy dose of stacked synths and bass lines to create thick and complex-sounding productions that ramp up the energy of the room or festival that the track is being played in. You can say what you want about electro, but it is the style that pushed EDM into the mainstream during the past couple of years.

If you want to get an understanding of what electro is, simply listen to anything by Wolfgang Gartner, deadmau5, Lazy Rich, Hirshee, Chrizz Luvly, Felguk, Dirtyloud, Vodge Diper, or my group, the Banger Bros. When you listen to material by the artists listed above, just make sure it says "Electro" on the style it was released under.

> **Examples:**
> Wolfgang Gartner—"Flashback"
> Lazy Rich—"Brainfreeze"
> Hirshee—"Big Life"
> Vodge Diper, Ryan Enzed—"Reckless"
> The Banger Bros—"Beep Beep Boom" (Chrizz Luvly Remix)

Progressive House

As the name suggests, progressive house is yet another subgenre of house music. The style emerged out of the UK in the early 1990s and is a cross between proper house music and trance music, featuring synths and trancey sounds. Like trance music, progressive house tends to feature dramatic choruses and crescendos, and the tracks tend to be longer than most other genres. A couple of the early pioneers of the genre are Faithless and Leftfield. One of the best progressive house producers in the world is Eric Prydz. Dig a little deeper, and you'll find that Eric has a few aliases and creates music in different genres. One of his aliases is Cirez D.

Examples:
Eric Prydz—"2Night"
Nervo—"Hold On"
Nicky Romero—"Symphonica"

Techno

Many people believe that techno started in Detroit during the mid to late 1980s. But if you dig deeper and take a closer listen to the German band Kraftwerk, you will discover that it's more accurate to say that techno's origins are German, not American. Yes, it's true that Detroit techno created a particular sound, but Kraftwerk's influence came first and is undeniable. Initially, techno was a genre that featured repetitive instrumental music of a futuristic and robotic-sounding nature. This is certainly one of those genres that have evolved considerably over time. In the midst of its inception, a lot of early techno music sounded robotic and futuristic (Kraftwerk's "Numbers," cited below, is a good example of this). That sound then continued, and the bpms (beats per minute) ramped up quite a bit. Somewhere along the line, Americans wrapped all EDM into the category of techno. Today, techno's characteristics tend to feature deep and dark bass lines and melody hooks.

Detroit Techno

Although techno originated in Germany, I mention Detroit techno here, and it's important to share a bit more about this genre because it did and does have a big impact on the EDM culture. In essence, Detroit techno was inspired by the concepts that Kraftwerk developed in the 1970s and '80s, some funk elements, and a sequencer to bring it all together.

Examples:
Juan Atkins, Model 500—"Times Space Transmat"
Carl Craig BFC—"Evolution"
Kraftwerk—"Numbers"

Trance

Germany is widely considered to be the home of trance music. The style was developed in the late 1990s, and it features tracks that are melodic in their nature. In fact, trance is considered to be the most melodic genre in dance music. Trance is anywhere from about 115 to 150 bpm and can include elements from many music styles, even classical and cinematic. Trance is generally uplifting and often features female vocalists who sing with an ethereal style.

A few of the trance icons are BT, Paul Van Dyk, Tiësto, Paul Oakenfold, and Armin van Buuren. Listen to most of their productions, and you'll get a great sense of what trance music is all about. Tiësto has broadened his production style into the realm of electro a bit these days, though. My personal favorite out of these artists is BT. He is a true pioneer, and during his live sets, he often plays live instruments and synths. Even though he's received many accolades over the years, I still view him as one of the most underrated artists in EDM.

> **Examples:**
> Humate—"Love Stimulation" (Paul Van Dyk Remix)
> Tiësto—"Adagio for Strings"
> Underworld—"Born Slippy" (Nuxx Remix)
> Armin Van Buuren—"Waiting for the Night" feat. Fiora (Beat Service Remix)

Dubstep

Contrary to what many Americans believe, the origins of dubstep come from London, England, back in the late 1990s. Dubstep music is inspired by genres such as drum 'n' bass (jungle), two-step garage, and broken beat. Often dubstep features a wobbly bass line effect with syncopated rhythms and tuplets. The bpm range is around 140. Like most EDM genres, dubstep embodies a fusion of a few different styles. Skrillex's sound defines one particular production style, whereas Bassnectar represents another. One of my favorite current techno producers by far is Nicole Moudaber.

> **Examples:**
> Carl Cox—"Chemistry" (Nicole Moudaber Remix)
> Rudebrat—"Won't Stop"
> Schoolboy, James Eghert—"Stardust"
> Skrillex—"Make It Bun Dem"

Glitch-Hop

Glitch-hop merged as a movement out of Germany in the mid to late 1990s. The style often features tracks that intentionally use manufactured CDs skipping, vocal chops, and the stutter effect, which was pioneered by BT. Glitch-hop is often extremely syncopated, with lots of abrupt starts and stops in the music. Although the movement started in the 1990s, one can trace its inspiration back to the early twentieth century to the futurist Luigi Russolo, who composed the song "Esempi Sonori Di," which was constructed from noise generators. A couple of the direct pioneers of glitch-hop are Aphex Twin and Autechre. This is one of those genres in which some of the productions sound similar to another genre. Can you guess which genre? Okay, time's up—it's dubstep.

> **Examples:**
> Aphex Twin—"Windowlicker"
> Autechre—"Clipper"
> Defunk—"Big Momma T"

How DJs Listen to Music

"I feel humbled and fortunate to have pursued my passions in life, and I'm grateful to have been able to travel the world, doing what I love." –Randy Seidman

DJs listen to music differently than the average music listener. There are two basic ways we DJs listen to music. The first is listening from the standpoint of how a particular track will sound in the context of a set, and how the flow of one track will fit next to another. This approach can be categorized as critical listening, because you are listening for how you can use a certain track in your set. How does it sound in the middle of a set? How do the instruments of a particular track sound next to the sounds of another when mixed together?

The second basic way a DJ listens to tracks occurs during the act of mixing. One of the most challenging things a DJ learns is how to listen to two records at the same time, while being able to decipher between them. How in the heck do you do that? At first the task seems daunting, but in time you will forget that it was ever an issue. As with many other things, the skill will become second nature with a lot of practice. Let's get you started on a technique that will send you on your way.

Listen to one track by itself very closely. Pay attention to all the details, instruments, and elements in the track. Listen to the sonic texture of the track sounds, as you pick out the verse and chorus parts. Can you distinguish all of the different elements, such as the various instruments, effects, and noises? Can you hear which instruments are introduced in the verse? What about in the chorus/hook?

Then try to focus on each sound. Listen to all of the different elements: kick drum, the bass, the synths, keyboards, vocals, and so on. Get to know each sound and all the instruments being used. Listen to not only what the key elements of the track are, but also when and where they are introduced. In most cases, tracks build up to a climax. The beginning and ending of tracks that DJs play during shows are primarily for mixing purposes to give the DJ enough room to mix in between tracks. This is why the duration of some tracks can be up to seven minutes long, or even longer. It's not that the entire track is seven minutes; the reason for this is all about giving you room to mix. Naturally, the beginning and ending sections will have the fewest number of elements happening to make for a smooth mixing and beat-matching process. It's much easier to mix tracks together when there is less going on in each respective track. When two tracks are at their peak, there tends to be a lot going on. If you are trying to mix with all that chaos happening, it is harder to hear each individual track. But creating mixing room that is sparse in its nature makes the job of mixing easier. Sometimes the beginnings and endings of tracks feature a simple kick and snare, other times it's the drums and noises. Just pay attention to the variations that different tracks have. But as I mentioned above, most tracks are sparser in these sections.

Songs are separated into instrument groupings. Paying attention to which instruments are being played where will help you familiarize yourself with how music is structured. If you are DJ'ing EDM, something to keep in mind is that although the sonic quality sounds much different from say a jazz trio or rock band, the general idea of the relationship that the different instruments have with one another is a similar concept. For example, in a rock band the lead guitar and rhythm guitar interact in a manner where both of their "voices" are heard. The lead will be featured most prominently, and the rhythm guitar will support the lead. An electro house track will also have a lead, but it might be a stack of synths, and instead of having a rhythm guitar, the producer might be using a different style of synth to support the lead. A rhythm section in a band typically consists of a drummer and bass player, and sometimes a rhythm guitarist. In dance music, it is all of your percussion elements, from kick, snare, and hi-hats to hand drums. The other part of this section is the bass line and/or synth bass. But sometimes the bass in EDM is considered the lead. Just use logic when determining which is which. The lead instrument is the one that is most prominent in the mix. It's important to realize that instruments are much like humans in that it's all about chemistry and communication. Some instruments work well together, while others clash and compete for attention. If a track is well produced, each sound fits perfectly in the mix.

Become as familiar as you can with listening to the different elements. Practice focusing on just the kick and snare for a while. How long is it playing during each section? The kick is your foundation for starting your mix, so make sure that you can find it quickly. The more you practice picking out the different elements and instruments of a given track, the more it'll help you with being able to decipher and distinguish between tracks. When a drummer plays a drum set, he or she needs to develop a skill called ear independence. This is where the right hand is playing a certain drum pattern while the left is doing something different, and each foot is doing something different from the hands. Ear independence helps you pick out various instruments while still being able to pay attention to the overall sound of the track.

Chapter Review

As you dig into the art and craft of DJ'ing, you will start to notice that you listen to music differently than most people. It's important to listen for which tracks will work well in your sets, and how each track sounds while mixing it with another. With this in mind, it's important that you listen to the sonic quality and structure of the tracks you listen to.

Exercise

Pick out a few of your favorite tracks this week and spend some time each day listening only to the tracks' specific structure, their sonic elements, and their relationship to one another.

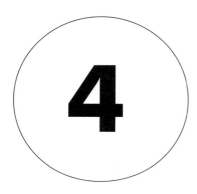

Establishing Goals

"We were fortunate to have been around since the early days of house music. Experiencing that fed a huge passion for being involved in the scene which has brought us to where we are today, with still a huge drive to see if we can re-create what it was like 'back in the day.'" —Prok & Fitch

N ow that you have learned some basic tools to get you started as a DJ, it's time to create your vision and look at setting some goals. I mentioned earlier that it's important to begin to inquire what direction you'd like to go in. Not to try to control the journey, but because the more clear you are with what you want to accomplish and where you want to go, the less time you'll waste traveling down roads that aren't really aligned with what you truly want. So with that in mind, what do you want to accomplish as a DJ/artist? Some of you might have a clear vision, while others have no idea. Either place is fine for now; your path will be revealed as you go.

But whether you choose to follow this dream or you have a different one, it is crucial to have a vision of where you are headed. At first, I thought I simply wanted to create electronic dance music (EDM) and travel the world. Looking back on it, I know that I had a vague sense of what I wanted, but it was not clear. A turning point for me was when a woman hired me to DJ for her fashion show back in 2006. Along with paying me a pretty handsome fee, she also agreed to sit down and do a consulting session with me as it pertained to my career. Her main job was consulting with businesses to help them create more success, so this was a nice bonus for me that I really appreciated. The things she said to me during our meeting that have stayed with me ever since were these simple but powerful questions. She asked, "Scott, what do you want to accomplish with your career? When someone comes over to your house when you are sixty, what are they going to interview you about? What have you achieved to that point? What was the story of your career and life?

Wow, I thought to myself. How in the world am I supposed to know what kind of things I would accomplish or be interviewed about? It was so far off into the future that I literally couldn't picture it. But this was the first time someone asked me something like that, so I knew the answers were in my head somewhere. Then she asked, what about ten years from now? What about five? Those questions seemed too daunting to even conceptualize, and my only answer to her was that I wanted my songs on the radio and that I wanted to play shows around the world. My friend then said, that's great, but the clearer you are with what you want, the better chance you have of achieving it.

So from that day forth, I started digging into my consciousness to find out what my true desires were. I journaled about five days per week on it for quite some time, and the answers started to come. As I discovered my true desires, I stayed true to them and have worked on being flexible in the process. And as I started achieving goals that I set, I had to refine my vision and think bigger. I remember a mentor once telling me, "Scott, you've got to think much bigger than you already are." During that time I had already had a big vision, but it was time to expand it. Each year my vision expands, and I remind myself to just stay in the flow.

Today, I am constantly expanding my vision. If you are vague about your vision, well that's exactly what is going to come back to you. If you're not clear with what you want, it's quite possible that instead of creating what you want, you will end up participating in someone else's vision. If you'd like to be among the few people who take the time to create the life that they want, then you are going to have to spend some time working with your vision on a daily basis. An essential part of my happiness and success has been my willingness to take a hard look at what I really want, then giving my attention and dedication to the pursuit of setting goals and defining my vision. I define what I want to achieve and I do what makes me happy. I go for it. I can't stress the importance of this enough. By creating a distinct plan of what you want to achieve in the music industry, your actions will be drawn to tasks that will move you toward these goals, you will notice that things will happen much faster for you, and you'll be happier in the process. The process of discovering your path is all about refining and experimenting. Be clear, be dedicated and decisive, and don't take yourself too seriously! If you realize that life is about having fun and doing what you love as often as possible, the journey will be smooth and fulfilling for you.

Did you know that about only 4 percent of the population write down their goals? But of the 4 percent that actually write down their goals and work with them daily, nearly 100 percent achieve their goals. Amazing, isn't it? This perfectly illustrates that as long as you stick to your goals and work on them consistently, the sky is the limit. As stated though, it's not enough just to dream and visualize attaining your goals; it's all about taking action in conjunction with visualization. Ever heard of the saying "You create your own luck"? Your DJ journey and life will be about what you make of it.

So you can't just write down your goals and forget about them. It's essential to be active and work on them every day. For example, I keep a goal book and look at it at least twice a day, and I spend time each day visualizing my goals as though they were already achieved. In fact, the first thing I do in the morning is to take an hour-long walk. During my walk, I first spend time being grateful for different things in my life. Then I spend the rest of the time visualizing the things I want to achieve as though they have already been accomplished. Visualizing my goals as having already been achieved sends the signal to my mind that they are already true. In the study of visualization and brain chemistry, it's a fact that our minds don't know the difference between the things we imagine and make up, and those we imagine that are already a reality.

Now, some things will take longer to materialize in the physical world than others. It all comes down to your belief in what you think is possible. So instead of filling your mind with worry, why not fill it with positive thoughts of the things that you'd like to achieve? Not only will this help you have more of a positive perspective, allowing your mind to learn how to expect the good things to come into your life, it will also help you achieve your goals faster. This is because the more you focus on them, the more energy your mind will spend figuring out how to accomplish them, and the more you think about what you want to achieve, the more inspired you'll be to take action to get closer to that particular goal.

But most importantly, I don't just visualize my goals happening—I work on them every day. My track isn't magically going to finish itself. This book isn't going to be written unless I sit down and write it. So, you have to do something about it. Visualization and writing down your goals is a big part of the puzzle, but the biggest factor is action. If all you do is fantasize about what you want, but you take no steps toward achieving what you want, very little will happen for you in that endeavor. But the starting point is indeed writing down your goals. Making your own goal book is simple. All you need is a notebook, and if you want, you can cut out pictures.

Write down your goals in a book or journal. When you write down a goal, write it as though it has already been achieved. There is a mnemonic goal system that I like to use, called SMART, which was developed by George T. Doran. The name stands for *specific*, *measurable*, *attainable*, *relevant,* and *timely*. Here's a quick breakdown of the system:

Specific. If you are vague, you are going to produce vague results. Saying you want to DJ all around the world is great and all, but the more specific you can be, the more of a positive impact it'll have on achieving the various goals you set. The more laser-focused you can be, the quicker and more efficient you will be.

Measurable. If you can't quantify and measure the goal, then you won't know how much progress you've made. Setting goals is about getting results, so to know if you are on target or not, you'll need a measuring stick.

Attainable. Is your goal something you believe you can achieve at this moment? You want to make sure the goal is believable to you. The more you achieve the goals you set, the bigger and bigger you will make them. I'm by no means saying to start small, but maybe the bigger goals that might take a while to achieve should be a ten-year goals—for example, taking over the world :)

Relevant. Is the goal something that is aligned with what you truly want?

Timely. Setting a deadline will help create urgency for you. There should be no panic or anything like that, but creating self-imposed deadlines tend to help you focus your attention on achieving the goal. What happens if you don't meet the deadline you set? Just push it back a bit.

Again, the idea here is to write your goals in the present tense, as though the goal has already been achieved. For example, instead of writing that you want to be a master DJ, consider writing, *I am grateful that by (month day, year), I am now a master DJ.* I would also recommend partnering up with a friend when it comes to goal setting. All you have to do is let this person know which goals you are working on and check in with each other either weekly or daily. Declaring to someone else and holding each other accountable to what you want to achieve will skyrocket your action level. I have an accountability partner that I speak to on Skype every week. Each week we talk about what we accomplished, and then we look ahead to the following week and what we want to create for it. We also try to e-mail each other Monday through Friday to give each other a quick rundown of the actions we plan to take during each day. I can't stress enough how much this has been helpful in completing my projects and achieving my goals.

Another important piece to goal setting is to categorize your goals as long-term or short-term. You could start by having a ten-year goal, a five-year goal, a one-year goal, a six-month goal, a three-month goal, a one-month goal, weekly goals, and daily goals. It's okay if you don't know what your exact goals are right now, but you should start defining them. I would recommend trying to set some, even if it's just for fun. If you are having a hard time thinking about some goals for yourself, here are a few examples.

- Today I am practicing mixing for one hour.

- Today I am writing for ten minutes about what I'd like to achieve with DJ'ing.

- By June 22, 20__, my mixes are spot-on, and the transitions between tracks are smooth and on time.

If you are someone who is struggling to define what you want, not to worry—you are certainly not alone! In fact it's quite common to think you don't know what you want. With some searching, though, I know you can find what you want because it is indeed inside of you waiting to get out. Spend time each day, a few minutes will do, asking yourself the question, "What do I want?" But instead of answering it, just ask it. Let it resonate, and ask again. Another way is to journal about it. You can use this technique while you journal. Write down your desires; write down the things you love to do. Your direction and vision is there for you; it's just a matter of your giving a voice to it.

Chapter Review

Setting your goals will allow you to take a look at where you are heading with your art. Doing so will also provide you with useful feedback about the progress you need to make, along with the progress you've already made. Starting to define your goals now will help you become clear with what you want to achieve. Remember, your goals and vision will probably change over time, so just inquire about what you want, write it down, and open yourself to what comes next.

Exercise

Your goals will evolve over time, but getting in the practice of setting them is an essential part of the process. Set aside ten minutes this week to write down one ten-year goal, one five-year goal, a one-year goal, and a six-month goal. If you aren't clear about what you think you might want ten years down the road, just write something down that you think you might want. If you are not sure which genre you want to DJ, you could set a goal of listening to two new artists per week, trying out all the different genres.

Bonus Exercise

If you'd like to go deeper with this, you can also write out one monthly goal, one weekly goal, and one daily goal. Keep working on these goals until you achieve them. Once you achieve them, check them off the list and move on to the next one. Make sure to write down goals that you can achieve. If your daily goal is to tour Europe all in one day, that's probably not going to happen. Create goals that are believable and achievable. You know I'm all about your dreaming big, so I'm not saying not to do that. I'm simply saying that the size of your goal will determine an appropriate time frame. And as you start to achieve your goals, you will gain confidence and be able to make them bigger.

Purchasing Equipment

"Follow your passion." —Nadja Lind

N ow that you've decided to become a DJ, it's time to go get your gear! This is both an exciting part of the process and a daunting one since the market is so oversaturated with equipment; it can be overwhelming when trying to figure out which setup is best for your needs. For some people it may not be, but if you are a newbie, it's likely that this will be the case. I know it was for me! Now there is so much gear and there are so many options that it can be hard to figure out which route is the best to take when purchasing new equipment. And all those channel strips and knobs on a mixer seem intimidating, don't they? Not to worry—as soon as you know what a channel strip does, learning what the rest do is a cakewalk because they all do the same thing on mixers. And getting the right equipment is actually simple and easier than it might seem, because we truly don't need all of the bells and whistles that magazine advertisements claim we do.

Unless you plan on throwing your own events and parties (which you might), you'll only need gear to practice and record mixes with for demos and possibly radio stations a bit later on. Why is that? Because pretty much all the nightclubs have most of the equipment you'll need for your sets. And if you get flown in to do a show, then you will have what is called a rider. A rider is basically a request for the gear and other things you need in order to do a show. Most clubs won't have the computer at the club, but as far as professional CDJs (a type of CD (a type of CD player that allows analog control of music from CDs), most establishments are equipped with them. If you are like me, you might get excited about all the gear that's out there, and rightfully so . . . many of us are gear junkies! For those of you who are not familiar with CDJs, they are a type of CD player developed by Pioneer Electronics that plays CDs and emulates vinyl control. Put more simply, instead of using turntables to DJ, you can use this type of CD player. But I can't stress enough that you need only the bare bones to get started. With that in mind, let's get into it.

I started making music in 2002, but I didn't start learning how to DJ until 2005. Back then, turntables were much more common than they are now, and a lot of DJs were still mixing with vinyl. A niche of DJs who mix with vinyl remains, so if you'd like to learn how to DJ the old-fashioned way, it's something plenty of DJs do. My setup at the time was hardware based, consisting of two Technics MK3s, a Vestax PMC-05 Pro 11 mixer, and Serato Scratch Live.

In retrospect, I'm happy with the route I went with my gear. Even though I never use vinyl anymore, it was nice learning how to mix on it because if you can mix on vinyl, you can mix on anything. Would I go back and change any of my purchases, though? Actually, yes—I would. Although the Vestax mixer is good and worked just fine, it's more of a scratch DJ mixer, which is not my style at all. I could've gotten a cheaper mixer for half the price. The PMC-05 is about $400. If you are planning on being a scratch DJ, then it's one I would recommend. A mixer that is designed for scratching features a functionality in its fader control that enables a DJ to manipulate the sound of the records by essentially flipping back and forth with the crossfader. A main concern here is that the faders need to be durable. Most of the time scratch DJ'ing is reserved for hip-hop DJs. If you want to hear a great example of how it sounds, do a Google search for DJ Q-Bert. If you do not plan on being a scratch DJ and are on a budget, I recommend the Stanton SMX.202. It's under a hundred bucks and provides all you need. Since I believe your home system just needs to give you the opportunity to practice and perhaps record some mixes, all you need is two channels, a cue, and outputs so you can run it through a recording device. The Stanton SMX.202 provides you with these things. As far as figuring out if you want to buy new or used, I think either is fine. I purchased some drum set equipment on eBay years ago and was very happy with the quality. Keep in mind, though, I bought cymbals. Electronics can be a bit fidgety with regard to their lifespan, but in general I think it's pretty safe to buy on a reputable online auction-based store such as eBay.

Since we are on the topic of fader and channel usage, below is a quick definition of each.

- **Channel.** A sound source travels into the mixer through an input channel. From there the sound is sent to the master fader, and out through the speakers. Your sound source as it pertains to what we are talking about would be your CDJs, or turntables, but in the live sound world it would be guitars, drums, vocals, and other stuff.

- **Fader.** The faders on your mixer's channels control how much of the sound is sent to the master fader. Faders can be a knob that rotates or a button that slides.

- **Crossfader/Xfade.** Usually located directly below the channels is a horizontal fader, which, if pushed to the right, will play sound only out of the channel on the right. If pushed to the left, only the left channel will play sound. And if you leave the fader in the center, both channels will play sound.

I chose to learn on regular turntables, but with many DJs making the shift to laptop DJ'ing, it's certainly not the norm to do so now. I look at it this way. The most common way budding DJs like you are learning is on one of the software-based mixing programs like Virtual DJ or Traktor. I use Virtual DJ for recording my radio mixes and have used it during a few live shows. I'm pleased with Virtual DJ and it works great. Although I finally decided to give Traktor a try at a show recently, and love it. You really can't lose with either one. But as far as their compatibility with external controllers, Virtual DJ is compatible with more devices. Obviously, this is a nice perk and it's an important one, as you will definitely want a controller if you choose to use the software while DJ'ing for clubs and gigs. With that being said, Traktor has the better reputation for being more durable and is generally looked upon as being the standard for professional DJs.

Learning to DJ on turntables is like learning how to drive on a car that has a stick shift. Can you get by with learning only how to drive a car that's an automatic? Of course you can—you are just limited in your choice of the kind of cars you can drive. And is driving an automatic still driving? Yep, last time I checked. If you learn to DJ only on a computer, that's fine because most DJs are doing that now anyway. There are a lot of people complaining about how laptop DJs are not real DJs. I find that quite funny because a while ago vinyl DJs were saying the same thing about CDJ DJs not being real DJs. And musicians have looked down on DJs for years, calling them nonmusicians and not giving them respect for their talents. So no matter what, there are always going to be naysayers. It's the whole "kids these days" syndrome. So once again, do what speaks to you and what inspires you, not what others might think of what you are or aren't doing.

I believe it's a waste of time to complain about how one is DJ'ing, because at the end of the day, the DJ's job is to play music and to entertain. Some of my musician friends think DJs are nothing more than a glorified jukebox. Is this true? Certainly not, but it's a reminder that there will always be people who try to undervalue what other people do. My only advice here is not to get caught up in this petty debate. Do what you like.

What I Use

As I mentioned earlier, most clubs are equipped with CDJs, a mixer, and a full sound system. I DJ mostly with CDs these days but have warmed up to the idea of using controllers, and am even getting back into vinyl DJ'ing as well. I do a weekly radio mix show for Berlin's Dance

Radio (PureFM), and record all of the sets via Ableton Live. So as far as what I use, below is the list of equipment that I own. Some of it is for production purposes, and some of it is for my live shows. Pretty simple, right? Sure—I could always have another toy, but I have absolutely everything I need.

- Ableton Live
- Apple Power Mac G5
- Djembe (an African percussion instrument)
- Drum mic
- E-MU Xboard 25 (keyboard/MIDI controller)
- Hercules controller
- Native Instruments Traktor, with S4 Controller
- Stanton ST.150 turntables

I used to play live shows with my computer and Serato Scratch Live, but during the past couple of years, I've been mixing almost exclusively with CDs. I prefer the minimal approach and not having to deal with setting up the computer. I also like that mixing CDs is closer to mixing vinyl than the computer is. I suppose there's just something sentimental about it for me. Plus, I think that when one uses a computer during a live show, there is a tendency to get "lost" in the computer screen, and you can forget that there is a crowd to pay attention to!

The Essentials

Your options are virtually endless when it comes to how much equipment is out there for you to choose from. But there's no need for you to break the bank when purchasing your equipment. This chapter outlines the basics of what you'll need to get started.

Laptop

There is an ongoing debate about what kind of computer one should use. Should you get a Mac or a PC? But the debate is endless, because depending on who you talk to, people have plenty of varying opinions about which one is better. I myself am a Mac user. I prefer Macs over PCs because I am more familiar with the key commands, and I like that they're more intuitive when it comes to trying to navigate through their inner workings. It also seems as though PCs catch viruses more often than Macs. Even though I recommend using a Mac, whether you are DJ'ing on a computer or creating music, it's simply about using a machine, PC or Mac, that's as fast as possible and includes as much RAM as possible. Mixing and creating music is a strain on your computer, so the faster and more powerful it is, the better.

Software Programs (Virtual DJ or Traktor)

Both of these programs are Mac and PC compatible. There are many other brands, but these two both have great reputations.

Sound Cards

Simply put, a sound card converts digital music files into an actual audio signal that can then be amplified and played out through your speakers. Sure, you can get a software-based program like Traktor or Virtual DJ running without a sound card. You can click on Play and the tracks will then play out of your speakers, and your PC's built-in speakers. But without a sound card, you will not be able to cue the next track you'd like to mix without it coming through the main source along with the one that is already playing! A sound card gives you two outputs: one for your main speakers, and one for your headphones. So, if you'd like to be able to practice mixing the way you will be doing during your show, having a sound card is highly recommended. Another great reason to get a sound card is if you are going to be producing music. I have a Focusrite Scarlett, and I'm very happy with it.

Mixers

I mentioned earlier that a mixer is a glorified home stereo system, but it is indeed more than that. In essence, a mixer allows you to combine different inputs of various sound sources, mix them together into a desirable effect, and then send the sound out through the output/speakers. If you are using a mixer in a live-band scenario, you might have four channels of drums, one channel of guitar, one of bass, and one vocal channel. The mix engineer would then mix and balance the level of each instrument channel, and voilà!— the crowd is enjoying the musical experience. With DJ'ing it's much simpler because instead of having to mix each musician, most of the time you just need to balance two channels. And of the channels that you are mixing, an engineer has already spent countless hours balancing each instrument and "musician," so the hard part in that regard is finished. But I digress, because live-band mixing is a whole other book!

The basic difference between analog and digital mixers is this: digital mixers are designed to emulate the functions of an analog mixer, and are equipped with faders, channel strips, and many other accoutrements. But with a digital mixer, all of your functions are programmable. You can set levels/volume controls or any other function and can recall the settings later. This can save you a lot of time. Think about it, if you had to tweak the levels and settings every time you turned on your mixer, it would, first, take time to do that, and second, you would have to remember your exact settings from before. Another great feature of a digital mixer is that since it's a software-based system, you have a massive number of inputs and outputs.

Inputs

Inputs are where you connect your sound source (that is, instruments, CDJs, microphones, and so on). Once a sound source enters the mixer, one of the first points of control is the input gain. If you look at the top of your channel strip, you will find the gain knob. This knob adjusts how much of the signal level from the sound source goes into the channel. As a general rule, you want to make sure to set the knob at a moderate level so you do not clip the signal. Ever heard a song that sounds like it's cracking and popping? That's what clipping is.

Don't worry, though, because even if you don't hear if a signal is clipping right away, most mixers have a meter that shows you when you are in danger of clipping. If you are pushing your meters all the way into the red, you need to back off a bit.

Common input connecters:

- 6.5 mm—For instruments such as electric guitars and other audio devices.
- RCA—For devices such as CDJs and some effects units.
- XLR—For mics and some audio devices.

Outputs

Outputs are where the signal is sent out of the mixer and through the sound source. Whether you send the signal out through speakers or through headphones, this is where the signal is introduced to the audience so they can hear the music.

With an analog mixer, you have a fixed number of inputs and outputs to choose from. What you see is what you get. These are just a couple of the main differences. Having more inputs allows you to plug in a controller and/or effects unit while you are DJ'ing on your system. If you have only two inputs, you won't be able to connect anything else other than your two turntables or CDJs. But if your home system is simply to practice on, then it's not essential that you have a 4-channel DJ mixer at home. If, however, your live shows will consist of incorporating instruments and controllers, then you'll want to make sure that the club is equipped with a mixer with enough channels for what you'll need.

With mixers, and just about any other piece of gear for that matter, it's important to realize that you can literally spend thousands of dollars on the mixer alone. If money is no object for you, then the $7,000 Pioneer SVM-1000 Audio/Video Mixer is one of the best on the market. But for those of you who are on a budget, the Stanton SMX.202 is a solid choice for what you need. Guitar Center sells them for about $70. You can certainly spend more on a mixer, but again, if you are using your home system only for practicing and recording mixes, you simply don't need to spend more than this on a mixer.

The debate about which medium is better is one that I don't think we'll ever have a definitive answer to. For the most part, DJs simply live in the digital world. With a big shift to a lot of DJs relying on their laptop and controllers, we are certainly living in a new era. My personal opinion about the main difference between the analog and digital worlds is that it is a matter of taste and depends on what you grew up listening to. Did you grow up listening to vinyl? Or did you purchase CDs? Or are you young enough to have only bought digital files? In my opinion, and the opinion of many others, you will tend to gravitate toward whatever your ears are used to, toward the medium you have heard most.

If you grew up listening to vinyl, then you're likely going to think that the analog world sounds better and "warmer." If you are a little younger, you'll probably think that the production quality of today's music is much better than it was ten years ago, believing that digital music sounds better. With that said, I am one of those people who believe that the sonic quality of today's productions sound better. To my ears, music today sounds richer and fuller of life, especially when it comes to EDM. If you compare an electro house or dubstep track to that of, say, an old '90s house tune, the latter is going to sound as though it were produced through a tin can compared with the beef of a massive dubstep track. But tell that to someone who grew up with the Beatles or Led Zeppelin, and you are in for a never-ending debate about why music in the old days sounds better and is of higher quality.

Ted, one of my good friends who is much older than I am, is a talented musician and sound engineer. Whenever he and I get into a discussion about the production value, it ends in a stalemate. He thinks I am wrong and that unlike decades ago, the kids these days just don't make quality music. There is an argument that the quality of vinyl sounds better than digital music files . . . that it's warmer. There are also many who believe that WAV files sound better than MP3s. Experts on sound have solid evidence to back this up, showing that the bit-rate depth of WAV files are deeper than MP3s, and thus don't cut off as much of the frequency range as MP3s do. I see their point, but I've also heard some experts mention that since we are not able to hear the full frequency spectrum, our ears can't really hear the difference. For a period of time I DJ'd with only WAV files because I believed that I could hear the difference, that the kick drum sounded and felt "thicker" to me. Theoretically, the human ear from the time of birth can hear frequencies between the spectrum of 20 Hz to 20,000 Hz. But just by living and being around typical sounds of the city (for example, car engines, horns honking, construction work, and so on) that range shrinks every year we get older. So, you know what? Even if the sound quality was a little better with certain formats, many people can't hear the difference.

I will say this, though—if it's a big deal for you to have the absolute highest quality of sound, then maybe you should DJ only with WAV and not even consider spinning vinyl. My opinion on the matter is that sound quality is like many other things: you get what you pay for. For example, if you purchase a cheap pair of shoes for ten bucks, they probably won't last long. If you instead invest in a moderately priced shoe for around $100, the quality is much better. But as you get into the extremely high-end shoes, the difference in quality between two high-quality shoes will not be all that different.

Moral of the story: don't DJ music that is so low quality that it sounds like mush. Mix quality-sounding music, both a 320 kbps and a WAV file are decent-sounding digital files. But if you are like some of my DJ friends (and me a few years ago), go ahead and play only the highest-quality-sounding formats out there. Nobody will complain about that, but just don't stress yourself out in the process! There are many who believe that if you are playing on a high-end sound system, the type of file you are playing becomes important because it is possible to detect the difference between WAV files and 320 kbps MP3s. My suggestion to you is to trust your ears. If you have access to an amazing system, crank some WAVs and MP3s through it and see which one sounds better to you.

Mixers, Turntables, and CDJs with Great Reputations

Mixers
- NU-SKOOL Rane Sixty-Eight
- Pioneer DJM
- Xone:92

Turntables
- Numark TTUSB
- Stanton STR8.150
- Technics MK3

CDJs
- Pioneer CDJ-1000s

Above are just a few examples of some mixers you can check into. As you can see, they can be quite expensive. Unless money is no object, I would recommend the Stanton SMX.202 or something similar. Have you ever seen or looked at a picture of a large mixing board? What the casual music lover doesn't realize is that once you know the functions on one channel, you know what they all do. This is true for DJ mixers. Even though some effects and functions may vary from mixer to mixer, they all pretty much do the same thing. Like anything you want to become proficient at, though, it's good to study different mixers just so you won't be surprised when you get to the club. Something I used to do before certain shows was to ask the promoter what kind of mixer the club had. When it was time to play my set, I wasn't surprised by anything, because I had studied that particular mixer and knew the basics about it.

Controllers

Even if you are just starting out, you are probably aware that a lot of DJ'ing is being performed using MIDI controllers. As with most other audio equipment, you have a ton of options to choose from. Below are a couple of choices that are great solutions.

Native Instruments Traktor Kontrol S4 has become the industry standard when it comes to computer mixing, and Native Instruments has some great controllers to go along with the software the company has developed.

Traktor's Kontrol S4 model is quite impressive and has everything you need with regard to mixing on your computer. It's a bit pricey, so if you are on a budget, you might want to check out the S2 model.

Pioneer and Reloop also create some great controllers. A quick Google search of DJ controllers should point you in the right direction.

All-in-One Controller

Stanton created the SCS.4DJ, the first truly integrated standalone DJ system that gets rid of the need for a laptop computer. So, if you don't want to deal with transporting a lot of gear and a laptop, this could be a great solution because all you need is your music. Stanton is one of the most solid DJ-equipment brands out there, and the SCS.4DJ has certainly been created on the cutting edge. If you want to check out more about this controller, the company site is www.stantondj.com.

More Advanced Gear

Now let's talk about some gear that is not necessary but is great to have if you can afford it. If you'd like to deck out your home-DJ setup with the best gear, below are a few examples of top-of-the-line equipment.

- **Korg Mini Kaoss Pad.** Essentially, this is a touch pad controller that comes with some great effects, making it perfect for live performances and some production work as well. It's a nice toy to have, but it certainly isn't necessary.

- **Pioneer CDJ-2000.** If you are planning on mixing with CDs and have the money, this CDJ is about the best you can buy. I am a fan of most all of the Pioneer CDJ series, and they certainly did not disappoint with the 2000s. These are the most durable and most accurate CDJ on the market. When I say most accurate, I am talking about the ability of the CDJ to keep the tempo locked in most accurately. This way when you are mixing, the tracks stay on time with one another much better than anything I've ever DJ'd on. The first time I played a show on a pair of them was in 2011 in New York City at District 36. I was blown away by how easy it was to mix on them!

- **Pioneer SVM-1000 Audio/Video Mixer.** Want to get into VJ'ing and DJ'ing at the same time? Pioneer hits it out of the park with the first audio/video combo mixer of its kind. In every industry there are companies that set a standard for excellence in their field. Pioneer is one of those companies when it comes to creating a top-of-the-line DJ'ing product.

As you can see, you can spend an endless amount of money on your equipment. If you are on a budget and just want to purchase enough equipment to get you going, then I recommend you pick up a similar setup to the one I referred to at the beginning of this chapter. I've read production books in which the authors would say something similar—about how it's not important to have all the latest effect processors and gadgets but instead it is more important to know your gear and maximize the equipment you already own. At the time of reading them, I remember thinking that I still wanted to get all the latest and greatest gear. Fortunately, I didn't succumb to buying a bunch of equipment I didn't need, but some of that was due to not having enough money. Thankfully, after gaining experience and obtaining success as a DJ and music producer without needing the newest toys, I've finally embraced the principles of truly maximizing the tools that I have. Hopefully, you get the message before going out and spending a fortune on equipment, because either way you spin it, the process will be expensive. But again, if money isn't a concern, then by all means pick up the best of the best.

I believe that a minimalist approach is the way to go. If I were starting out today, I would learn how to DJ on CDJs. What if you have a show at a club, and for some reason your computer crashes, or the Zip drive with all of your music is lost on the way to the show? If you've learned how to DJ with CDJs, then you can bring your music on CDs and you won't be out of luck if something goes wrong with your computer equipment. Pretty much all clubs have a pair of CDJs, so I highly recommend learning how to mix on them. If you do decide to mix on CDJs, it'll be good to have a pair at home so you can practice as often as possible.

If you want to get top-of-the-line CDJs, go for it. But I would recommend getting a pair of cheap CDJs for two reasons: first, it'll save you some money; second, if you can mix on a crappy pair of CDJs, you can mix on anything. Imagine you've got that first big break and you are playing at one of the best nightclubs in your city. You arrive to the club and to your delight the DJ booth is armed with a pair of brand-new Pioneer CDJ-2000s. These are top-of-the-line and mixing on them is about as easy as it gets. If you end up mixing with CDJs, you will find that keeping your tracks traveling at the exact same tempo is one of the challenges you'll face. The 2000s are so precise that the tracks you are mixing don't drift apart from one another nearly as much as they do with any other CDJ. And since you've been mixing at home with the less-than-reliable CDJs, it'll be smooth sailing riding with the shiny Pioneers.

Chapter Review

When purchasing gear, remember to keep it simple. There are endless options out there with regard to which gear to purchase. But do you really need all the bells and whistles? Whether you are going to mix with your computer, CDJs, or turntables, you don't need to go overboard with trying to get the latest and greatest.

What kind of musical format do you want to mix with? Do you like vinyl or digital formats? Whichever you choose to DJ with, just make sure the quality is good, but there's no need to nitpick.

Exercise

Write down one list showing the exact setup you would get if money were no object. If you are on a budget, then write down a second list showing the kind of setup you are looking to actually purchase. This setup will contain only the equipment that you need. Your first list will be a dream list and something you can work toward, purchasing equipment as you save money. The second list is the one you will be acquiring soon. This exercise will help you determine what you need as opposed to what you desire.

Setting Up Your Equipment

> "I was mesmerized by the way that one person could make so many people move in unison and create happiness among the dance floor." —David Carvalho (WhiteNoize)

The amount of time it takes to set up your gear and what you'll need depends on the type of equipment you have and your experience using it. If you are running a software-based system, such as Virtual DJ or Traktor, your setup will be extremely minimal. In this situation it's simply a matter of installing the software and connecting the sound device via USB or FireWire to your computer. If you want to run the sound out of the speakers instead of headphones, then you'll need to set up your sound card. At first this process seems difficult, but it's actually pretty simple—just check in with the directions.

If, however, you have a hardware-based system complete with a mixer, CDJs, and/

or turntables and your speakers, your setup will be a bit more involved. But once you get the hang of if it, it's straightforward. Connecting gear is all about making sure that your signal path lines up in a way that the signal flows from the sound source out through your speakers. *Signal path* is the flow of the audio signal in, through, and then out of your mixer. One example of a particular signal path is music coming out of your CDJ. The audio signal travels into the mixer via an input, down through your channel strip, and out through your main outputs. Both the hardware and software installations have simple dos and don'ts. As long as you read the setup instructions, it shouldn't take you long to get up and running. I recommend that you at least become proficient at setting up your gear, because although a lot of clubs have a sound engineer to assist you with certain aspects of the setup, it's expected that you know what you are doing when it comes to setting up the gear that you bring into the club. Quick note: Make sure to be nice to the sound engineerhe or she is your best friend before and during the show.

After you've opened your brand-new equipment, it is a good idea to read the setup manual. If you are anything like I am, then you are not a big fan of reading manuals and like to just get in there and figure it out on your own. But with sound equipment it is important that you look over the manual before setting up your equipment. Once you have done this several times and are comfortable with the process, many of the systems you will purchase from here on out will probably have a similar setup with regard to the equipment being ready to run. Once you've gotten pretty good with setting up your gear, it'll become second nature, and when you purchase that new piece of outboard gear, you'll be able to set it up in no time. But when in doubt, read the manual!

> **Important Note:** As you start playing gigs out at clubs and festivals, it will become increasingly important to take good care of your equipment. The wear and tear on gear comes even from simply using it at home, so when you are gigging, it's especially important to take good care of your equipment. Buying equipment can be expensive, and the better you take care of it, the longer it will last for you. I remember seeing a good friend of mine's Avid Mbox (which uses Pro Tools software), after a show. It looked like he had thrown it on the ground and jumped on it a few times. Needless to say he needed a new one. So make sure to slow down and handle your gear with care!

Chapter Review

At first, the process of setting up equipment can be a bit of a pain, so it's important to read the manual before trying to mindlessly put everything together. I recommend learning as much as you can about the inner workings of the kind of gear you will be using, because the more you know and the more experience you gain with setting up equipment, the more it'll feel like second nature.

Exercise

Research a piece of equipment that would be a dream come true if you owned it. Is it the best mixer on the planet? Do you have an extraordinary sound system that has enough juice to power an outdoor concert? Whatever it is, use Google to find the setup manual. Once you have it, read through its steps to get familiar with the setup process. Another thing you could do if you just purchase new equipment is to take out the manual and go over the installation process. This might be boring to some, but the process is worth it and you'll thank yourself later. The more familiar you are with setting up equipment, the more valuable that skill will be during your shows when there are equipment issues and someone needs to solve it.

Sourcing Music

"A great DJ knows how to channel energy from what they're feeling in their head into the minds of those on the dance floor!"
—Richard J. Dalton (KNHC - C89.5 FM - Seattle, WA)

As a DJ, the best place to purchase your music is Beatport. There are other online stores such as iTunes, Djtunes, Track It Down, DJ Download (now a part of Juno Download), Stompy, and so on—but in my opinion, Beatport is the best. It all depends on what kind of music you want to DJ. If you love deep house and old-school house, then Traxsource and Stompy are great stores as well. Sometimes a particular store might not have the track you are looking for, so you might need to dig around in the others. I always start with Beatport, and if it doesn't have it, then I'll check the others. Beatport often has the exclusive rights to sell releases from many of the best labels during the first two weeks of a given release. This means that during the exclusive period, no other store has the possibility of selling the release until the period is over. Sometimes it's a two-week exclusive, and sometimes it's longer—it just depends on the deal that the distributor and label work out with Beatport. Most DJs and producers from around the world know this so they tend to shop at Beatport first, knowing it is the most likely store to shelve the latest tracks first.

The way I see it, Beatport is basically like the iTunes for DJs. Most consumers purchase their music on iTunes, whereas most DJs buy music from Beatport. Even though I am partial to Beatport, the relaunch of Djtunes is creating quite a buzz right now, so it will be interesting to see what happens because it is a great place to get music as well. Especially since you are starting out, I recommend that you search for your music on as many sites as possible. This will give you a good idea of what kind of music you can expect to find on each respective site, as they are not all created equal. Plus, it will be a great way for you to explore as much music as possible. As you learn exactly what you are looking for, you can narrow down the sites you visit. Let's take a deeper look into the stores that I find to be the best right now.

- **Beatport.** This online store definitely has a strong reputation in the DJ world and is known for being one of the best, if not the best DJ download store out there. Its interface is the best in my opinion, and it has many of the tracks you are looking for. If there is a negative about Beatport, it's that it is a little more expensive than Djtunes.

- **Djtunes.** This store has had some nice buzz going on about it lately. And people are saying that it has the biggest and best music collection out there.

- **DJDownload.com (JunoDownload.com).** This is another great download store that has a wide range of dance music. Its EDM catalog is immense, so you'll find many great releases here. My complaint with this store also comes down to its interface. The music player interface is not as good as Djtunes' and Beatport's, because when you click on a track to preview it, it opens up in another window and is sometimes slow to load.

- **Stompy.** This store holds a warm spot in my heart because this was the first place I used to search for tracks. Stompy was started in San Francisco, and it features all things underground house. If you want that Chicago-style house, this is the place for you.

- **Trackitdown.** Early on in my DJ career this is where I went to get most of my tracks. There's an emphasis on European-based music, and it has a big selection of releases. One complaint I have about this store is that the music player seems to get bogged down and can be a little slow at times.

As you search for your tracks on different sites, you will notice that you gravitate to some more than others. The best way to find out which online store is best for you is to dig through the options.

Another way to get your music is to sign up with a record pool. Many record labels send their music to record pools to help promote their releases because a good record pool will have a great network of DJs who they send new music to. Many record pools cost money to belong to, but some of them are free. And if you get yourself in position to be a tastemaker DJ, record pools will approach you because labels want you spinning their tracks because of your influence on the music industry. A tastemaker DJ is one who is considered to have an influence on what other DJs play. If a big tastemaker is playing a track, it often creates a ripple effect in the scene. When other DJs find out a tastemaker is spinning a tune, they will want to play it as well. Many tastemaker DJs have radio shows, which gives them access to a wide audience. Being in a record pool can give you access to releases before most of the general public. This is a great way to get new music before the common music consumer. Do some research and find some free DJ pools to sign up for. Below are two great DJ pools. I use both of them to help promote my releases. Even if you live in a country that is outside of the areas I listed in the record pools below, not to worry. Since record pools mostly send digital files, they are able to reach anywhere in the world.

- **Starfleet Promo (United States).** Starfleet Music Pool (www.starfleetmusicpool.com) is a record music pool that includes some of the hottest club, mixshow, *Billboard*, mobile and mixtape DJs, plus professional remixer/producers throughout the USA, Canada, and around the world. It has built up a strong reputation in the EDM industry as being a great resource for artists and labels to get their music to many of the tastemaker DJs from around the world. I have worked with the pool on several releases and am very pleased with how it helped expand the audience of my music.

- **Kings of Spins (Europe).** This record pool (www.kingsofspins.com) has been in operation for ten years and has offices in the USA, UK, and EEC. It is another solid option for getting your music into the hands of the right DJs around the world.

Some of the other top record pools include the following:

- **Kings of Spins Masspool.** A respected DJ pool, Masspool (www.masspoolmp3.com) has a variety of EDM and hip-hop.

- **ZipDJ.** This record pool (www.zipdj.com) has a great reputation and has a wide range of releases across many genres.

The best way to get your music is by receiving promos from your favorite record labels or artists, directly. It's similar to a record pool in that labels send out their upcoming releases to DJs who they think will have a positive influence on their releases. This will happen for you as you network and develop relationships in the industry. Most of the time, record labels will get in touch with you and add you to their promo lists. If labels and DJs see you as someone who has influence, they will reach out. That's not to say you can't reach out to them as well. In my opinion this is the best way to build your library because you are often getting unreleased "secret" weapons that won't be available to most DJs until the official release date. And you are getting these secret weapons from your favorite labels, so obviously most of the releases will be those that you look forward to playing. How exactly do you do this? There are a number of ways to go about it. I'll start with an example that shows how I got on my first promo list.

Story

American house music icon DJ Dan was one of the DJs who inspired me to become a DJ. A friend of mine saw me perform in Seattle in 2006 and later mentioned that I should connect with DJ Dan, because she thought my style fit with his. Fast-forward about a year, and I ended up meeting Dan by chance while attending Burning Man. We had a brief and friendly interaction about our mutual friend, and a couple of months later Dan ended up signing my and my music partner's first single, titled CyberSutra "Lick It." Upon signing our track to Dan's label, InStereo Recordings, they added us to their promo list. To this day I still receive their promos, and it's still one of my favorite promo lists I am on.

The next several promo lists I was invited to were on record labels that I signed music to. Today I am on a bunch of record pools and promo lists from various labels and record promotion companies. I am not sure how I got onto a lot of them, and sometimes I get a little frustrated because many of these people didn't ask me if I'd like to be on their list. Don't get me wrong, I'm grateful for it because I take it as a compliment that these groups want me one their promo lists. I just wish they would have reached out to ask if it was okay, first.

To recap the story, a great way to get on a promo list is to sign some of your music to a label that has a promo list. Another way is if you have a radio mix—either Internet based or FM. If you have a mix show that is respected, DJs and labels will want you to promote their upcoming releases on your show. Another way is to create a podcast that becomes popular. Achieving one or a few of these things might seem as though it will take a long time, but if you are focused on and intentional about your actions, it can happen faster than you think.

Obviously, you have to build up trust to receive music from other producer and DJs, because when they send you their music, they are trusting that you won't share it with random people. They will want you to play it on a podcast, show, or radio mix, but they won't want you to be giving it away to your friends. Even with illegal downloads being rampant in today's music world, there are those who still operate with integrity in that if someone trusts you to keep a track to yourself, they know you won't be giving it away mindlessly.

So when starting out your career, it can be difficult to get on these lists because they are reserved for DJs who are considered "tastemakers" by the label or producer who is sending them out. But how are you going to find out if you can get on an exclusive promo list if you don't ask? If you can convince the label that you are trustworthy and that you can help promote them, they might be willing to send you their exclusive promos. Sometimes all it takes is getting in touch directly with the source and asking them if they can include you on their promo list. If you visit the label's site, you should come across contact information that'll point you to the appropriate person. If the label has just one contact option, it's safe to say that you can just get in touch that way. Other times a label will have their staff members listed. If that's the case, keep an eye out for positions in promotion and marketing. If you don't see that option, just send your message to whomever you think would be the appropriate person—the founder, for example.

Yet another great way to get music is if you own a record label. You might want to wait to launch it until you have gained some experience in the industry. For example, my music partner and I reserved the site Golden Needle Records (www.goldenneedlerecords.com) back in 2007. We had the idea to start a label back then but didn't feel ready until 2010, which is when we launched it. It might seem daunting to own a record label, and there are certainly a lot of steps you have to take to launch it. For example, you will need to trademark the label, write a business plan, and register your business with the state that you are doing business in. But if you've always wanted your own label, why not research about how to get it going? I started my own label, called Golden Needle Records, because I wanted to have another platform to release our music. I wanted to have more freedom and flexibility when it came to what I wanted to do with my releases. And one of the many benefits of having my label is that there are quite a few producers around the world sending me demos and free music. So along with all of the other options, it's a great way to get new music as well.

Chapter Review

When I first got into listening to electronic music, I was overwhelmed by the amount of genres there were to keep up with. Something I tend to take for granted now is that it's easy for me to pick out genres. I used to reach out to my friends in the industry to ask them about a particular genre, but now they come to me because I have dedicated myself to learning as much as I could about electronic music. I still have a lot to learn, but because I took it upon myself to be educated about electronic music, I have a good grasp on what separates the music soundscapes.

Exercise

Take time this week to look at the top ten tracks of each genre on Beatport's website. Pay attention to what differentiates genres from each other, and take a few notes to help you capture some of the differences.

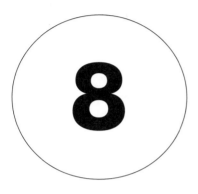

Scheduling
Practice Time

"A great DJ has charisma and taste for good music. They reads the crowd's mind and give the people what they want." —Gary Caos

Scheduling your practice time is very important. Some of you may love structuring your time, and others not so much. I've participated on both sides of this fence and found it much more effective to schedule things out. A great method I learned is to fill out my calendar at night before I go to bed. I write in the things I want to do the next day. By writing them down at night, my mind already begins to think of completing the actions. It's a powerful way to help you act on the things you want to accomplish. If you are feeling really inspired, you can schedule out your week. Organizing your entire week gives you an advantage in following through on the things you want to accomplish.

You might be asking yourself the question, Why in the world do I need to schedule anything regarding my desire to be a DJ? It's really quite simple: to be good at anything takes discipline and focus. To excel at anything, one needs to prepare and practice as much as possible. But if you aren't one for structure, not to worry—you don't have to be hyper-organized to practice . . . perhaps you can find another method that works for you. I would recommend giving the method I suggest a try, and if it doesn't work, you can always ditch it and go back to how you were doing it before. One of the most effective ways to create success is through repetition, so whether you schedule your practice time or not, you'll need to do plenty of practicing. So find a way to schedule at least some practice time.

When starting out, I recommend you spend at least one to two hours of practice time per day. But as I just mentioned, you don't have to schedule your practice time— just make sure that you do practice. So whatever method you choose, just make sure it's one where you practice a lot.

As I said in the introduction, I pursued a professional baseball career. I was usually the guy on the team who was the free spirit and tried to get by with my natural talents as much as possible. But even I knew that I played much better during the times when my focus and attention were directed toward getting better. Those times were few and far between, so I definitely didn't maximize my talents and become nearly as good as I could've been. But making that mistake was a great lesson for me when I was starting out as a DJ and music producer. I knew that if I wanted to be great, I had to put the time and effort in to be great. Did I become proficient at the craft of discipline and focus overnight? Of course not, because discipline and focus (like many things) are learned behaviors. Too many people believe that discipline and focus are traits that we are born with. That's not true at all; they are both qualities that we can strengthen and develop. But if you commit to them, in time they'll be comfortable and natural. With all that being said, below is how I schedule my time.

My Schedule

I used to simply schedule my days out the night before, writing down and mapping out the activities I wanted to accomplish. But a few years ago I came across another system, so now I break my days up into what are called *focus days*, *buffer days*, and *free days*. I learned this approach from reading Jack Canfield's book, *The Success Principles*. I highly recommend it.

Focus Days

At first this wasn't the case, but I now have three focus days per week: Tuesday, Thursday, and Friday. Focus days are days in which you focus 85 percent or more of your time on your core genius. The other 15 percent is filled with anything other than what your core genius is. For example, if you own a record label as I do, you could be sending contracts, reaching out to remixers to remix upcoming releases, and so on. And what is your core genius? For me it is the part that is producing music, playing a live show, writing, editing this book, producing my radio show for Berlin's dance station, and producing my record label's podcast. Whatever you excel at is a good indication of what your core genius is. What are the things you have the most fun doing? That's probably a core genius of yours. The main point of a focus day is that most of it is spent on your best talents. All other distractions should be put aside.

Buffer Days

Buffer days are days in which we prepare for focus days and handle the day-to-day operations of whatever business you may be in. For me, a buffer day consists of organizing and putting together releases for my record label, sending out my promo material, getting in touch with a public-relations agency, and organizing upcoming productions I have going. Right now I have a couple of promotional companies that I hired who send out my release promos to radio stations and mix show DJs. But before I was able to do this, I did most of it myself. It costs money to work with record promoters, so if you are tight on cash, a great way to accomplish this is to do it yourself. Believe me when I say that it's not easy promoting your own material, but if you don't do it, who will? Besides, by reaching out to radio stations and tastemaker DJs, this gives you an opportunity to build relationships with them. To this day I still send out my promos and network quite a bit. The more people you have sending out your material, the better. Even if you have a promotional company sending out your music, you can never have enough people doing this, so I still send my material to radio stations and DJs around the world.

Free Days

These are days in which you do absolutely nothing pertaining to work. The idea here is that you totally unplug and relax. This is a great time to take a hike, go to a movie, or just veg around the house. Whatever you choose to do on these days, just make sure it's fun and relaxing and not work related. The reason this sort of strategy was developed is because studies have shown that people who stick to this type of system of taking off one full day during the week are more recharged for the upcoming week. By taking off one complete day, you allow yourself to completely replenish. While editing this book I've noticed that I got away from doing this, so I've got to get back to taking time off during the week, because I feel more productive when I give myself a day to recharge my batteries.

> **Important Note:** With regard to this scheduling system, I realize that many of you work or are in school, so it won't be entirely possible for you to stick to this system right now. But don't worry. Even if you just have one focus per day or dedicate part of the day to one, it's going to make a difference for you. Just do what you can.

A couple of other great methods to help you create momentum and build upon your successes are also from Jack Canfield's book. At night before you go to bed, write down five things you did during the day that got you closer to your goals. Did you practice? Even for four minutes?

Write that down. Did you research DJs to send your music to? That's another one, and so on. The sheer act of doing this makes you want to do more of the same. Each day builds on another, and you begin to create a life designed around powerful actions toward your vision. You see, most of us have negative thoughts about the things that we didn't do during the day. This not only has a negative effect on our mind, but it also causes us to procrastinate more. Logging your successes of the day combats the negative flow of energy with action.

The other tool that is valuable is called "the evening review." You can do this while lying in bed. Just before falling asleep, scan over your day and look at the actions you took. Sometimes you will notice that you wasted more time than you wanted or didn't get enough done. Simply observe this without judgment. Then, play your day back in the way that you would have wanted it to go. This not only helps erase the negativity around what you might have slacked off on, but also, as you do this, helps train your mind to get used to doing the things you want to accomplish throughout the day. Before you know it, the evening review will be more aligned with the actions you set out to take. The final step of the evening review is to look at the upcoming day. Visualize all of the actions you want to take and see yourself completing them. Visualize yourself creating flawless mixes, with each transition being smooth and in time. Repetition is the ingredient of greatness, my friends, so have fun with these techniques and watch your skills soar through the roof.

Below is an example of the schedule I use.

Monday

- Take a 1-hour morning walk (hour of power visualization).

- Answer the e-mails in my inbox. Send out 5 press releases. Contact DJs about being featured in podcasts.

- Practice drums for 10 to 20 minutes.

- Practice keyboards for 10 minutes.

- Create music for 2 hours.

- Write book for 10 to 20 minutes.

- Record my weekly radio show for Berlin's dance station.

- Organize releases for Golden Needle Records.

- Do my evening review.

Tuesday—A Focus Day: This means that at least 85% of my day is spent producing music and writing.

- Take a 1-hour walk (visualization).

- Practice drums for 10 to 20 minutes.

- Practice keyboards for 10 minutes.

- Answer e-mails. Listen to demos. Send out 5 press releases. Contact DJs about being featured in podcasts.

- As soon as I've completed the previous tasks, it's time to create music or compose for an extended period of time.

- Go to the gym.

- Edit my book for 30 minutes.

- Produce music for an additional 2 hours.

- Do my evening review.

Wednesday

- Take a 1-hour walk (visualization)

- Practice drums for 10 minutes.

- Practice keyboards for 10 minutes.

- Answer e-mails. Listen to demos, send press materials out to magazines, and/or outsource to PR firms.

- Organize Golden Needle Records releases. Send out contracts. Send promos to DJs and clubs.

- Go to the gym.

- Produce music for 2 hours.

- Do my evening review.

Thursday—A Focus Day: This means that at least 85% of my day is spent producing music and writing.

- Take a 1-hour walk (visualization).
- Practice drums for 10 to 20 minutes.
- Produce music for 4 hours.
- Answer e-mails and send promo materials.
- Go to the gym.
- Edit my book for 30 minutes.
- Produce music for an additional 2 hours.
- Do my evening review.

Friday—A Focus Day: This means that at least 85% of my day is spent producing music and writing.

- Practice drums for 10 minutes.
- Produce music for 4 hours.
- Answer e-mails and send promo materials.
- Edit my book for 30 minutes.
- Produce music for an additional 2 hours.
- Do my evening review.

When I first started this system, I didn't think I had enough time for more than one focus day per week, so I started with one focus day, on Fridays. Shortly after starting this particular program, I added another. Finally, I added three focus days, which is where I am with it now. This feels like a good number—but again, it took some time to get up to that many. The same is true for my hour walk in the morning: in no way did I think I had enough time to take a one-hour walk five to six days per week. So, I started out by walking each day for fifteen minutes, and within two weeks I was up to the full hour. The reality of time is that we do indeed have enough time. If we are not getting most of what we want done during the day, it's likely because we are wasting too much time. That's certainly been the case for me.

Chapter Review

There's a misconception that artists tend to be people who are scatterbrained and live an unstructured life. Although we all have different styles with regard to completing work projects and making sure that we improve our skills every day, the discipline of practicing to become a better DJ or any other skill is essential. The practice schedule I've suggested in this chapter will help you stay focused on improving your skills as a DJ. If you are absolutely unable to stick to a schedule, just make sure that you find time daily to practice. It's not important that you practice at the same time every day; just make sure you give a lot of attention and energy into making yourself a great DJ.

Exercise

Set aside one day this week where you spend at least 80 percent of your time focused on your core genius. Make sure that it's on a day when you don't have school or work. For some of you it might be the weekend. Whatever day you end up choosing, make sure that most of your day is focused on DJ'ing, creating music, or whatever else you are most passionate about. At the end of the day, journal about how it felt to focus most of your time on the thing that makes you happy.

Envision Your Success

> "A great DJ is someone who comes from love, possessing the power to summon the atoms of red giant stars and the cosmic dust of all existence into the hearts of the audience, returning everyone back to the source at that present moment." —SpekrFreks

Take time out of each day and act as though you've already achieved the goals you've set and that you're the superstar you aspire to be. Don't have any desire of becoming a superstar? Then just visualize whatever it is that you'd like to be. Maybe you simply want to DJ great parties for a couple of friends. If that's the case, visualize your friends having a great time dancing and your set being flawless. Whatever your goal, take time out each day to envision it as if it were already a reality. Visualization is crucial to achieving success. Even if you don't think you are visualizing, you already are doing it without realizing about it.

Ever envision something that is to happen in the future as going well, or are you ever fearful that it could go wrong? The imagery you are using during these times is visualization. Your mind doesn't know the difference between positive and negative thoughts, so the more you visualize seeing yourself as having already achieved your goals, the more likely your "daydream" will become a reality. It's a case of faking it until you make it, and it will pay off. Visualization is something that I practice daily, and it is a big part of my success. The reason I bought into the concept of visualization when applying it to my DJ and music career is that, while I was playing college baseball in Arizona, I read a book called *The Mental Game of Baseball*, by H. A. Dorfman and Karl Kuehl. In the book the author discussed the topic of visualization and how the top Olympic and pro athletes around the world all utilized its power. Upon reading about the techniques in the book, I decided to give it a try and soon saw that I was playing my best by far when I was practicing visualization on a regular basis. One particular season I was a visualization fanatic, and it was my best season. It works.

Some people may try to tell you that achieving your dream is not possible. Well, I am here to tell you that they are absolutely wrong! It's important to realize that if anyone is telling you that you can't achieve something, it's most likely because they are stuck in their own life with regard to what they think they can and cannot do. They might have good intentions when they tell you your dreams are not possible, but that doesn't matter. These are people you should not listen to. I've had many people over the years say I wouldn't be able to do something that I was intending to do, only to have a few of them later admit to me that they were wrong to doubt me. It was actually big of them to admit that they were wrong, and I appreciated them coming to me years later. But you won't get that kind of courtesy from most people who doubt your dreams.

I mention the previous point not to pat myself on the back, but to share what was an important lesson. I learned that there are many people who default to looking at what is not possible, and, naturally, they will not be able to see what could happen down the road if they were to apply themselves. Some people can see only what is right in front of them. Visionaries can see possibility. I believe that if you have dreams and aspirations, then you are among the visionary folk. I've learned along the way that there are certain people whom I can trust when it comes to sharing my dreams and aspirations, and others I can't. Today, I share my dreams with only those whom I know will be encouraging and supportive.

There are just two reasons that people do not accomplish their dreams. Either they give up too soon, or there is something better in store for them. That's it, folks. It isn't because they aren't talented enough, old enough, or young enough. You can learn everything you need to be successful. Just stick with it no matter what, and you will get to the promise land. And if your dreams take you in an unexpected direction and it feels good, just go with the flow and things will work out even better than you originally planned or thought possible. There was a time that I thought I was literally put on this earth to play baseball. I was devastated when my baseball career came to a close, but it was one of the best things that ever happened to me. Keep that in mind as you travel along your path of chasing and attaining your dreams.

If a guy who used to be so messed up in his addictions can achieve the things I have in music and now with my career as an author, then so can you. Not too long ago, there was a time in my life when some people didn't believe that I would still be alive, let alone doing something worthwhile on the planet.

So, my friends, I say, go for it. No matter how big or crazy your dreams sound to anyone, you can do it. No matter how big or small your vision is about DJ'ing—or anything else for that matter—it's all possible. The most important thing about your journey is to have fun and do what you love to do. Once you start your process, be prepared for an amazing journey that, if you stay dedicated to it, will grow into something even better than you can imagine for yourself now.

Chapter Review

As you start to implement the tools available to you in this book, your vision for what you want to become as a DJ and an artist will become clear. Many of us spend too much time visualizing things we are afraid might happen. Since your mind is already in a state of visualizing, why not help guide your thoughts and images toward a direction that's more desirable? Many of the most successful people and the best athletes in the world practice daily visualization. Want to help skyrocket your success? Practicing visualization is a powerful tool that will help you skyrocket your vision.

Exercise

Spend fifteen minutes this week visualizing a perfect day. If everything were lined up exactly how you wanted, what would your day look like? For example, one of my perfect days would be the following:

- Wake up, do sit-ups and push-ups, go on a morning walk.

- Come back and eat a great breakfast and drink some coffee.

- After breakfast, head downtown to do a couple of interviews—one local, and another with *DJ Mag*.

- Come back to my hotel room and go over last-minute preparations for my show later that night.

- Take a nice hike around the area, come back, and eat dinner. Relax for a couple of hours, and then head off to the venue to hang out and socialize.

- Play a rockin' show, where everybody is having a great time and my mixes are spot-on every time.

- After the official show, play an underground show until six in the morning.

- Come back to the hotel room and go to sleep.

This is just one example. Use your imagination to create your own.

Imagine that you are right now the DJ you want to become. Imagine that you have achieved the things you are dreaming of. Set aside time to write down the things you've accomplished. Once you have, take a ten- to fifteen-minute walk, visualizing that it's all true. How does it feel? What is your confidence level like? Go into as much detail as possible, and focused only on visualizing your dreams being true now. If you drift off, just bring yourself back to the visualization. Bring an iPod or iPhone and listen to music without lyrics, so you can stay focused.

Part II

The Craft

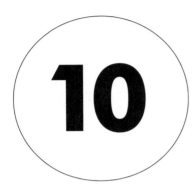

10

Mixing Basics

"To me, there are three things that make a DJ great: technical ability, track selection, and heart. They're like pieces of a puzzle, and if one of them is missing, you're left with a two-legged donkey, which is no good for disco." —Vodge Diper

N ow let's move on to the mixer. As previously mentioned, seeing all of those faders and knobs can be daunting at first. But think of your mixer as a glorified master volume control unit similar to your home stereo, iPad, and so on. Yes, of course, it has more functions than this, but at the most basic level of mixing, this is going to be how you get the sound out to the crowd. A mixer serves the function of blending tracks together and distributing sound out into the world. There are several different types of mixing techniques, and which genre you are spinning will determine the way you will mix.

For example, in house music, you generally hold your mixes together for at least one minute. By "hold," I mean that they are both mixes are playing in time together. The fades between songs can be abrupt or more gradual, depending on where the track is coming in.

If you want, you can mix so there is an abrupt change between the tracks, or you can create a smooth blend on the fade. Play around with both and experiment with how each of them sounds in different tracks. In hip-hop the mixing is essentially a cut stop, in which the first track changes quickly to the tune you are mixing in. A hip-hop DJ set is a chain of abrupt transitions from one track to the next. It's evident to the listener when one track is finished and the next begins.

In contrast, trance and progressive music is generally a gradual process of mixing, blending the two tracks seamlessly into one another. Trance is one of the genres in which mixes tend to be held longer than some of the others. Since trance is often melodically based and sometimes minimal in the spacing of its instrumentation, it can be fun to experiment with creating one song from your two separate tracks. For example, say one track has a synth that you really like, and the track you are mixing in has a bass you love. Experiment with blending the tracks together to feature these elements in the main mix. Remember, it doesn't have to be trance music in order for you to experiment with swapping instruments of each track. You can try this with virtually any genre. But if you are going to do this, it's important to mix tracks that are in the same key, or else your mix will clash. But nevertheless, this is a fun way to mix.

Like anything, learning how to mix in key takes practice and, of course, knowledge of the various keys in music. Once you learn all of the keys of the music scale, you'll start to recognize when you are mixing two songs that are in the same key or if they are off. Even if you are not able to identify the exact key, you will certainly be able to hear when they are not in the same key, because it'll sound off. So even if you are not knowledgeable yet when it comes to this, you at least can tell when keys are clashing, because they simply sound strange when played together.

If you want to take a shortcut, you can use a software program called Mixed In Key, which labels the key of the tracks in your music library. Obviously, I recommend that you learn how to do this by ear as best you can, because it'll strengthen your skills as a DJ and an artist. Many professional DJs around the world use Mixed In Key, so there's no shame in using it. And I see no problem with using Mixed In Key, because it can still help show you how things sound when they are in key. You can use it as a tool to help you learn keys. If you are anything like I am, though, you are going to want to learn how to detect the key of a track without having a software program do it for you. When I attended music-production classes in college, part of the program was dedicated to music theory. I can't stress enough how glad I am that I learned the basics about music construction, because it gave me a solid base of musical understanding.

As I continued to dig deeper into learning about chord structure, key signatures, and music theory in general, detecting what key a song is in started to get easier. I'm not saying I'm an expert, but even if I am unable to examine the exact key of a track upon listening to it, I am certainly able to detect when keys are clashing and which tracks work with one another based on whether they are in a major or minor key. The *Alfred's*

Essentials of Music Theory book series also comes in a great software version to get you started on your journey of studying music theory. There are many books and software programs available out there that can get you going; Alfred's software program is one I learned on in college, and it got the job done.

Mixing is an art form, but to truly take advantage of the freedom of your mixing style with regard to where you will start your mixes during a track, it's important to know song structure. Once you know song structure, you will be more comfortable with where to mix in and if you want your mix to be an abrupt transition or to be more gradual. When I was starting off, I would sometimes mix in the middle of a 16-bar musical phrase or passage. For example, instead of starting my mix on the 1 of a 16-bar phrase, I might start it on bar number 4. Not sure what a bar is? A *bar* consists of four beats of music and is also called a *measure*. For example, when you hear the kick drum beating like a heart (1, 2, 3, 4), that is the equivalent to one bar.

I am one of those artists who like to spin a variety of music. With my DJ group, the Banger Bros, the focus is on electro house, dubstep, and progressive house. And lately with my solo project I've been diving into some proper house, funky house, tech house, and techno as well. When I'm mixing I generally use three different methods, each with a different starting point, when getting ready. The first method is when track 1 is playing in the breakdown section. At this point I'll cue up the second track and get ready to beatmatch. The reason for this is that the breakdown is the point in the track at which the energy level goes down. The basic purpose of a breakdown is to give the listener a "break." It's designed to keep things interesting and to give the listener a change so he or she won't get bored by hearing the same thing for too long. Once track 1 goes back into the chorus after the breakdown, I will start record 2. This starts your mix at the beginning of the chorus or hook phrase. When mixing with this method it's important to know your tunes, because with most breakdowns there are not any drums to help keep time when lining up the mix. You will need to time it right when the first track hits into that chorus.

With the second method, I wait until after the last chorus/hook section is played out before mixing. For example, when the song goes into its last chorus after the breakdown, I will wait 32 bars to start my next mix. Again, this starts the mix at the beginning of the musical phrase, because most all tracks are constructed in 16-bar chunks. This is my preferred way of mixing because the main chorus/hook of tracks has a lot going on instrumentation-wise, so I feel that mixing while they are resolved creates more space and dynamics in the mix. There are no rules here, but you definitely want your mix to make sense, so you will at least want to start your mixes at the beginning and end of a phrase. It wouldn't make sense for the audience to miss a third or half of a vocal or synth hook, would it? If you are watching a good movie, you want to watch the entire film, right? This is the same with music, so make sure you deliver the full "picture" to the people on the dance floor.

Chapter Review

The kind of music you DJ will determine the amount of time you'll hold your mixes. If you are going to be a hip-hop DJ, you will not need to hold your mixes for long at all. If, however, you will be spinning trance tracks, you'll hold longer mixes. But with most EDM tracks (even trance), you don't have to hold your mixes for longer than one minute, sometimes even less if you choose. The more comfortable you become with holding your mixes, the more fun it can be. But it's nice to know that you don't have to hold mixes for too long if you don't want to!

You can use Mixed In Key or another software program that will ensure that you are DJ'ing tracks that are in matching keys. There is nothing wrong with that, but in my opinion, it's much better to learn music theory. The more you learn about music, the more satisfaction you'll have. Not to mention, you will become a better DJ because of it!

Exercise

- Pick out a couple of tracks in the various genres you are thinking about DJ'ing in. During your daily practice this week, focus on mixing with these particular styles. Notice how different one style is from the other? What are the challenges of each genre you are mixing?

- Look up the definition of a musical key this week. Examine a C major scale. How many notes are in it? What are its notes? Interested in learning more? Research books and software programs and purchase one. You will thank yourself for it later.

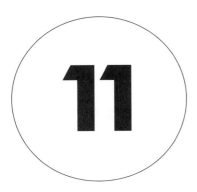

Beatmatching

"What makes a DJ great is their ability to be a channel of universal love. Great DJ'ing goes beyond track selection, mixing, and stage presence. When a great DJ plays, dancers lose all of their ego boundaries and are lifted up out of their physical beings into a transcendent state of bliss." –DJ Eric Sharp

Now that you are starting to think of what kind of DJ you want to be, let's talk about the basics of *beatmatching*. Beatmatching is playing two tracks at the same time while keeping them at the same speed. Mastering this aspect of the craft is one of the keys to being a good DJ. At first this seems daunting, but let me fill you in on a secret that may put you at ease. You don't have to hold the tracks in time for an eternity! Being able to hear if both of your tracks are in time and going at the same speed takes time. Practice speeding up and slowing down records on purpose so that you can start to notice when one is going faster or slower than the other. Below are two examples of how to adjust your track.

The Bump Method

If you are DJ'ing with turntables, the record is played on top of what is called the platter. You can adjust the platter by speeding it up or slowing it down in order to move your track back in time with one another. But this will keep the records in time only briefly, because it does not adjust the master tempo of the record you are adjusting. CDJs have a similar function, but instead of using a platter, they have what's called the jog dial. Because this method adjusts the tempo of the track only temporarily, just use it to get your tracks lined up tempo-wise, then make an adjustment with the tempo controller.

The Tempo Control Method

The tempo control is located near the bottom right of most turntables and CDJs, and next to the virtual turntables in software programs. The best way to adjust the speed of your tracks is by adjusting the tempo. Be careful when using this method, as you will not be able to tell if your adjustment is exactly accurate right away because it takes the tempo controls a little bit of time to make the tempo adjustment. Therefore, you might have a tendency to make too large of a tempo adjustment if you don't hear an immediate difference in the speed change. With that in mind, if you feel as though your tracks are pretty closely in time together, make minor adjustments and be patient.

When you're starting out, there is a tendency to adjust the tempo of the track with the bump method because there's an immediate gratification of the tracks seemingly being in exact time together once you bump it forward or backward. I highly recommend you perfect adjusting the tempo of your tracks by mostly using the tempo control, because it's the only way to ensure that the two tracks are playing at the same tempo. Think of the bump method as the starting point from which you can make final adjustments. Practice speeding up and slowing down a track by using the tempo controls only.

Some people like to hold long mixes. In most forms of EDM, you need to hold the tracks together for only between one to two minutes. This is especially true in the main genres of EDM, such as most versions of house, or trance. Depending on the exact tempo, it takes most of these tracks about one minute to resolve the full 32-bar phrase. So in most cases, you can hold your mixes for approximately one minute. Just make sure that this timing lines up with the tracks you are mixing. As I've explained, most track structures are similar in a particular genre, but sometimes they are a little different. Obviously, you can hold them for longer if you'd like, but it's not usually necessary. And remember my advice for mixing in 32-bar chunks: if you hold your mix for longer than that on the first chorus/hook section, you'll be beatmatching into the breakdown section. It's not that you shouldn't do this; I just don't recommend it, because a main function of the breakdown is to give the listener a break from the groove. This is a resting place, so to speak. I often edit out an entire breakdown section because there are no beats in it. People are there to dance, so because a breakdown is usually a low-energy place in a track, people on the dance floor get bored and stop dancing. Do you want that? Nope!

With that being said, sometimes people need a short break from dancing, so I will strategically place tracks that include a full breakdown, just so I can give everybody a quick breather. With practice and patience, before you know it, you will be holding your mixes in your sleep!

Beatmatching is a big part of what DJ'ing is all about. In my opinion, doing it is the most fun thing about being a DJ, but at the beginning, it's also the most challenging. It's very satisfying when you have both of your tracks playing at the same time and everything is lined up nice and tight.

Here's an exercise to help you practice beatmatching:

- Pick two identical tracks. This is a great way to start, because you know that these two tracks are going to be the same tempo. It'll be much easier for you to tell if you are perfectly on or not.

- Make sure that the track has a prominent kick at its start, because it'll be easier to find the first beat. Some tracks have melodic intros before the kick starts. With these tracks, it's more difficult to line up and find the tempo of the two tracks you are mixing because the beats have not been introduced.

- Now set your mixer so that track 1 is playing out through the main mix and track 2 is in your headphone cue. The main mix is what the audience can hear, or if you are practicing at home, it's what you can hear in your room.

- Play track 1. Find the kick in track 2 in your cue, and begin to move the track back and forth in time with your first track. If you are mixing on a computer, you will not need to move the platter back and forth; all you'll need to do is click on Play when you are ready.

- When you think you have the two lined up, let it fly! You are now beatmatching!

Quick Tip: DJ'ing is all about rhythm and timing, but it's easy to get into your head too much because you are trying to make sure you have all of your controls set up properly. To simplify beatmatching, pretend that you are dancing. You can tap to a beat on time, can't you? Well this is no different; it's just dancing with your hands. Even if you can't dance, you can tap to a beat on time as you probably do it quite often while listening to music. When I am timing my mixes, I often will tap my finger on the side of the CDJ. This way I stay in rhythm with the tracks I am mixing, and my finger is on the trigger, so to speak.

Chapter Review

Beatmatching is quite possibly the most difficult aspect of DJ'ing, especially if you are mixing with turntables or CDJs. Perfecting this aspect of DJ'ing will take time and practice, so it's important to be patient with yourself. And if you can remind yourself that you don't have to hold your mixes for eternity, that will take some pressure off and you can focus on the fun of keeping your tracks in time. You don't need to pole vault over an anthill. Yes, it'll take you time to perfect this skill, but it'll happen sooner than you might think if you just stay fluid with your motions while mixing. Relax, my friend—this is what DJ'ing is all about.

Exercise

Hopefully you are smack in the middle of your daily DJ practice. If you are, you can incorporate the next actions into your daily practice routine.

- Practice starting to beatmatch immediately after the breakdown of a track.

- Then practice beatmatching at the end of the 32-bar phrase after the breakdown. Remember, the easiest way to count it out is to chop it up into two 16-bar phrases.

- Practice speeding up and slowing down a track using the tempo control fader only.

- Now practice speeding up and slowing down a track by using only the jog display (CDJ) or the platter (turntable). See how this does not keep the tracks in time with one another?

Cueing

"Good DJs play great music without playing the obvious—
they play what people need to hear, not so much what
they want to hear." —Jordan (The Crystal Method)

In the UK, if you are waiting at the checkout line in the store, you are "waiting in the cue." This is essentially what cueing music in your headphones is about. You are listening to the track in your headphones before you play it in the mix with the track that is being played on the main speakers. This gives you an opportunity to figure out where you want to start mixing on this particular track. It's a great place to test the waters before you introduce the track to the crowd. Sometimes I'll do a quick test mix, just to make sure I've got everything lined up where I want it.

- Prepare two tracks so that they are ready to play.

- Set the crossfader on your mixer so you can hear one track out through your main speakers. The crossfader's function is to implement smooth volume fades from one signal source to another.

- Adjust the cue control on your mixer so that you can hear the track in your headphones and the master speakers.

- Put your headphones on one ear. Set your cue so that you hear track 1 in the main mix and track 2 in your headphones.

- Pay attention and to listen to each track that is playing. Mixing is being able to hear both at the same time, and this is exactly what you are doing now.

The Split Cue

The split cue function allows you to hear the output of your mixer in one ear and the channel/ track you are not cueing in the other. The split cue allows you to hear both of the tracks you are mixing in your headphones. A great thing about this function is that you can mix entirely in your headphones without the need of speakers. Mixing in the headphones is something that I do often; the only minor problem is that you don't have the luxury of hearing how your mix sounds in the room. Once you are confident in your abilities, however, you will know where your levels need to be and this will not be an issue.

Most mixers should have a split cue function. Usually, the cue is located next to the left volume fader, but it depends on the mixer. The cue function is a key component to mixing, so you will be using it often. Again, this allows you to hear both tracks in your headphones or to audition one track with the other playing on the main speakers.

The Cue

This is the most basic way to cue your track; it means to start your track on the beat and in the place that you desire. Most of the time this means starting your track on the first downbeat of the track. Usually, this comes from the kick drum and is the first sound you hear in a given track. Use just one turntable or CDJ, playing in your main mix. And if you recall from previously, I mentioned that it's critical that you start your mix at the beginning of a musical phrase. Now let's apply this knowledge and take some time to practice these techniques.

- Play track 1 out through your main speakers.

- Select a track that has a prominent kick. For those who need an introduction to what a *kick* is, it's short for *kick drum*, which is the drum that is triggered by a drummer kicking a peddle with a beater attached to it (sometimes called the bass drum).

- Now find the first beat of the track. This will be the first kick sound that you hear. Hold the beat right there, by grabbing the platter of the turntable and literally stopping the record from spinning. If you are using CDJs, you will not need to hold it, unless you choose to. CDJs do have a function that emulates the function of a turntable, to the point of being able to scratch if you'd like. With both CDJs and laptop-based mixing devices, you can click on Pause to stop the track. So instead of holding the track in place the way you would need to do with a turntable, you'll simply click on Play/Pause.

- If you are using record turntables or CDJs, move your track back and forth at the same tempo that your track 1 is playing in the main mix. Once you feel like it is in time with track 1, let it go.

Quick Note: If you are mixing with a software-based program, instead of moving the turntable or CDJ platter back and forth, simply click on Play on your computer.

Fading

The next facet of mixing is fading. Again, there are different methods here. The basic method is to bring the fader up on the track you are introducing into the mix, and fade out the other track. How fast you transition in and out will determine how smooth or abrupt fade-in or fade-out will be. If you would like to create a smooth transition between the tracks, then you will fade each track slowly. If you want an abrupt change, then you'll be more aggressive with your fading technique. It all depends on what kind of effect you want to create on the dance floor. Another method is to "fade" by EQ'ing. By cutting the bass frequencies of track 1 and boosting your second track, you will create a fun effect.

EQ'ing tracks is the function of manipulating the sound of a track by boosting or cutting the desired frequency of a given track. If you want, you can cut all the frequencies of the track you are mixing out. You still will have volume playing out of that channel, so I don't recommend fading in this manner. But this method is the way to swap one bass with the other—something to keep in mind when mixing and DJ'ing. How is the way you are mixing going to affect the dancers on the dance floor? Even if you don't like to dance, you've likely been on the dance floor before. If you can recall a couple of different DJs, what were some of the things that separated a good DJ apart from one who lost his dance floor to the point where people stopped dancing? Mixing transitions are extremely important, because the good DJ will keep the flow moving in his or her mix. Fading between tracks is a big part of this.

Within these methods of fading there are many ways to achieve your fade-in and fade-out. Experiment by doing them slowly and quickly. I use the first two examples the most. It completely depends on the mood of the mix I want to create on the dance floor.

How to Use Your Faders

- With the crossfader in the center position, you can use the channel faders to bring the volume of one track up and the other down. This is the way that I mix, because by leaving the crossfader in the center position, I don't have to worry about remembering to move the fader each time I mix in a track. This way it's ready to go. From here, it's simply about bringing up the fader on the track I am mixing in. The basic difference between the crossfader and the channel fader is that the crossfader fades the volume between one channel to the next. If the crossfader is set in the middle on a 2-channel mixer, you will be able to hear both channels equally. Move the crossfader all the way to left, and you will be able to hear the left channel only. The channel fader controls the volume level only of its channel. In most cases, the crossfader moves horizontally and the channel fader moves vertically.

- Some people like to move the crossfader to the left or right, depending on which channel your track is playing on. For example, if I have a track playing in channel 1 (the left fader), once I am ready to mix in the second track, I can move the fader to the center position. After I mix in the track, my cue track will now be channel 2 (the right side). Now I would have the fader slid all the way to the right, and would repeat the process of moving the fader back to the middle when I am ready to mix in. This method is quite common and has a nice flow, but I prefer method 1 because it involves fewer moving parts.

- With both crossfaders up, you can move your crossfader to the left and right to determine which record will be sent to the main mix. I don't recommend doing it this way because sometimes you might forget which channel you are mixing on and accidently bring that track into the main mix. The result? An absolute train wreck!

- Using the fader is an art and a craft. I use method number one nearly 100 percent of the time. There are no rules about how to fade, but just remember that you are trying to achieve clean mixing, so experiment with volume levels that achieve this the most effectively.

Although it takes practice to create smooth and accurate fades during your mixes, let's not make this too complicated. We've all adjusted the volume on our home stereo, yes? This is essentially what your fader control is all about. It's all about creating smooth transitions while you are mixing two songs together. If you are listening to music with your friends—whether it's in a car or at your home—you want the music played at a volume that's loud enough so you can hear it, but not so loud that it hurts your ears, right? Using the faders on your mixer is similar in that you want your audience to enjoy the music at a loud-enough volume.

But if you are erratic with your fader volume control, it'll interrupt the crowd's listening/dancing experience. For example, if you mix in a track at a much higher volume level than your track that is already playing, it'll throw your audience off. Keep things smooth and on point, just like with your home stereo. It takes more practice to perfect it, but the concept is similar.

Obviously, the more you practice the better you will get, and before you know it, these techniques will become second nature as well.

Exercise

This exercise is one in which we will build up through three stages, because it's about developing and sustaining your practice time. When building your "practice muscle," it's unlikely that you'll be able to start off practicing one to two hours per night. So, with that in mind, below are the three stages:

- Spend ten to fifteen minutes practicing the mixing tips illustrated in this chapter. (Two weeks)

- Once you've completed the first two weeks of practice time, spend the next week practicing for thirty-five to forty-five minutes per day. (One week)

- During the last phase, we are going to ramp it up. This is where the rubber meets the road and is what separates you from the crowd. From here on out, practice for one to two hours per day. If you can do more, go for it!

Song Structure and Music Basics

"A good DJ is someone that tells his story like a prophet but has the sensitivity to feel the crowd, and possibly leans to one or the other direction depending on the situation." —Miro Pajic

Music Basics

Although it is not a requirement for a DJ to have formal music training, knowing some basics can really help. With that being said, it's imperative that you learn at least the song structure of the genre of music you are DJ'ing. Why? Because knowing the song structure is how you will know if you are mixing at the beginning of a phrase or halfway into it. I encourage anyone who is studying the art of DJ'ing to learn as much as possible about music theory and song structure, as this will only make you more knowledgeable and, in my opinion, a better DJ.

It's true that as a DJ if you just want to do the bare minimum, you will only need to learn when you should begin playing your new track into the mix. But it would vastly improve your craft and marketability if you were to learn things like harmonic mixing, theory, and song structure. Most DJs today are also music producers. If you are even thinking about the possibility of creating your own music, then learning as much as you can about music and music structure is essential.

Harmonic Mixing

What is *harmonic mixing*? Harmonic mixing occurs when you mix two tracks together that are either in the same key or have keys that share the same key signatures, ensuring that they will go well together. Each song is created in a certain key of a musical scale. Some songs are created in a major key, and some are in a minor key. If you play two songs together that are in a different key, it sounds horrible to the trained ear. Even to the untrained ear, it will sound off. And although the audience won't necessarily pick up that the two songs are in different keys, they will know that something doesn't quite match up.

What Makes a Key Major or Minor?

A *major scale* is one of the most commonly used scales. It is made of up eighth notes, and one note in particular (the root note) is included twice. The eighth note in the scale is one octave apart from the first note of the scale. There are eight steps in a major scale. Each key on a piano represents one half step.

Below is a list of the scale degrees:

1st—Tonic (root)

2nd—Supertonic

3rd—Mediant

4th—Subdominant

5th—Dominant

6th—Submediant

7th—Leading tone

8th—Tonic

The more you know about music theory, the more flexibility it will give you. I have a lot of DJ friends who have had no formal music training, and they not only get by, but excel. But why limit yourself? DJ'ing is all about timing, song flow and energy, so you can become quite good without formal training. Heck, John Lennon didn't have "formal" training, and look where his career went. Paul McCartney did, however, end up teaching John a lot of what he learned, and Paul was formally trained. So although you don't need to have formal training, the more you know about music in the sense of how it's created and structure, the more equipped you will be as a DJ/artist. The more you learn about music, the better!

Experimenting with the technique of *modulation mixing* is another great way to change the energy on the dance floor. For example, if you mix a track in that is a half step or whole step on the chromatic scale above the track that is already playing, your dance floor will experience an exciting shift in energy. The chromatic scale is a musical scale made up of twelve pitches.

Song Structure for EDM

All songs have a specific structure. In pop music, one of the most common structures consists of an intro, verse-chorus, verse-chorus, bridge, chorus, chorus, and finally the outro. Dance tracks are structured into four main sections: an introduction, breakdown, back to the main section, and the outroduction. I imagine each music piece as a sonic story. In every story there is a beginning, a middle, and an end. When you watch a movie, the script will take you on a journey that builds your emotions to a climax and takes them back down to a resolution. Some movies create a slow and steady build to the peak of the story, while others are more dynamic and dramatic. It's the same concept with music. Some songs are fast, some are slower, while others are funky or bluesy. Songs elicit many different kinds of emotions according to the genre or theme of the piece, but nonetheless, they all have a similar structure that is followed when creating EDM. Below is a snapshot of the basic structure of EDM.

- **Intro.** An intro is 32 bars long. In EDM the intro is used for mixing room. The intro consists mostly of drums, percussion, and light musical effects. The reason that there is not a whole lot going on in this section is because this is where you will be playing two tracks at once. Producers give DJs space to mix here so there isn't the potential for a lot of instrumentation clash. You do not want the incoming track to compete with the song that is already in the mix. This is not always the case, though. Sometimes tracks get quite busy, even in the intro section. Just make sure to know your tracks, because if one is extrafull and busy from the start, you'll need to be mindful of where you start mixing it in against your track in the main mix.

The other main reason for the intro section is that all songs—whether pop, country, rap, dance, or rock—have a beginning, middle, and an end. Imagine if a movie consisted of only the climax. Even though that might sound like it would be intense and exciting *all* the time, our minds are such that we would get bored if that was all we saw. Music is all about dynamics, and keeping the listener engaged. The intro is the perfect way to set the beginning of the song up.

- **Breakdown I.** A breakdown is 32 bars in length. The breakdown is the section in the track when the dynamic energy of the song comes down a bit . . . sometimes to a screeching halt! The purpose of this section is to give the listener a break from the hectic synthesizers and heavy bass lines. Most of the time a breakdown is very laid back in contrast to the rest of the track. The concept of the breakdown is to change things up so that a track is not boring and keeps you engaged. Our attention spans are short, and if you were to listen to the same melody for the entire length of the song, you would get bored and stop paying attention to what you were listening to. A breakdown within the song structure gives our minds something else to focus on, and it gives us a needed break. When the song comes back into the main section, the high-energy contrast creates an element of surprise and excitement that we are back into the hook. Please note—not all breakdowns are 32 bars. Some are even longer, and others are 16 bars. You might be starting to see a pattern though, right? Everything is created in 32-bar chunks. A producer can cut that down to 16 bars in a breakdown if they'd like, but you'd be hard-pressed to find a track that is created with 13 or 15 bars.

- **Main Section I.** The main section is 32 bars. It is the meat of your song and is equivalent to the chorus in pop music. It's the place in the track that you remember, even when you are no longer listening to it. The main section is the most memorable part of the track and is where the hook happens; it's where the magic happens. What's your favorite tune right now? Can you hear it in your head? That's the hook, and your mind is probably recalling the chorus/hook section.

- **Breakdown II.** The second breakdown is 32 bars.

- **Main Section II.** The second main section is 32 bars. After the breakdown, the song will go back into the main section that was introduced before the breakdown. Oftentimes there will be minor augmentations from the first main section of the tune that are reiterated in a different way in the second main section. For example, there might be extra synthesizers, pads, or vocals added in one octave higher than the lead synthesizer to create a harmony and element of higher energy. Simply creating a harmony in a higher octave, whether it's with instruments or vocals, causes a cool experience for the listener. It can be a subtle augmentation, but it makes the difference. The bottom line is that the second chorus/hook section is virtually the same as the first, plus some extra shine.

- **Outro.** This section is similar to the intro in that its main function is to give the DJ mixing room. This other main point of this section is to resolve the track. Again, most of the time this section consists of mainly beats, percussion, and some effects. You most likely will not hear main vocal parts or leads in this section. Sometimes more instruments and vocal chops are left in this section, but they are sparser than in the main section of the song.

Above is the basic structure of EDM, but you will find that songs vary a little depending on the type of genre. Or if the producer is trying to capture a particular effect, he or she might structure the song a bit differently. The example I mention is one of the most common structures these days when it comes to most forms of EDM. It's important to note, however, that the structure has changed a little over the past couple of years. Below is an example of how a lot of electro house tracks were formatted.

Intro = 32 bars

Main Section I = 32 bars

Breakdown = 16–32 bars

Main Section II = 32 bars

Outro = 32 bars

But for the most part, this is a typical example of EDM structure. A great way to find out the structure of song in a particular genre is simply to count the bars. The easiest way to do this is to count 32 bars of music at a time. You will discover additional structures the more you listen to different music and EDM genres. Each genre has a particular structure, and there are often a couple of variations. As you study the structure of a given genre, you will start to see that they follow a strict structure. The formula is consistent within each genre.

When to Mix

Many DJs like to mix using the "every 32 beat" rule, meaning that at the end of 32 beats you either want the track you are mixing in to be playing out through the speakers or you are getting ready to introduce it to the crow. It's ideal to have your mix start in at the beginning of a 32-bar phrase or at its end. If you come in during the middle, the timing of your mix will be off. Think of how you feel when someone interrupts you midsentence. Even if you don't mind it, it's still an interruption to you when you are trying to finish your thought. Or think about when you start watching a TV program or movie halfway through the episode. Eventually you might be able to piece together what happened, but by coming late you missed valuable content. It's the same thing in music; let your songs say what you intend before introducing another idea (song). And be on time.

Below is a common example of song structure in EDM:

32 bars of intro/mix in room

16–32 bars (breakdown)

32 bars of song's main chorus/hook section

16–32 bars (breakdown)

32 bars of song's main chorus/hook section

32 bars of outro/mix out

Here's a good way to chop it down even more. Each section is usually created in 16-bar phrases, and so a 32-bar phrase is essentially 16 bars repeated, with some variations, of course. Since you want to start your mixes at the beginning of each phrase, it might be easier to count out 16 bars instead of 32. In fact, that's the way I do it. Not all songs are structured this way. Sometimes a breakdown might be only 16 bars long. And sometimes the mix in or mix out length is longer or shorter than 32 bars. Something that you can almost always count on in EDM genres such as tech house, electro, techno, and house is that everything is produced in 16-bar phrases.

Pop Structure

As a DJ you will not necessarily be dealing with popular song structure, at least in the context of DJ'ing it in your sets. But it is always good to learn as much as you can, especially since a lot of really cool remixes and bootleg tracks are created from pop music. When pop songs are made into remixes, they follow the structure of the genre they are remixed in, but even if you are going to be DJ'ing them in, say, an electro house version, it's still valuable to learn what the song's original roots and structure are. Below is one of the standard song formats used in pop music. There are several formatting standards, so it wouldn't hurt for you to look them up and study them, but this will give you a sense of how pop music is structured. If you are looking for a great resource about songwriting, I highly recommend reading the book called *The Craft and Business of Songwriting*, by John Braheny. Again, as a DJ, it's not a requirement for you to learn about songwriting and pop structure, but if you plan on learning how to produce music, the more you can learn about songwriting, the better. And even though I produce EDM, I have found that reading the book listed above and studying the overall structure of pop music have enhanced my abilities as a music creator.

Pop music is structured into 32 bars. This is the complete song, so instead of there being four chunks of them (as I gave in the examples in EDM), this is the complete song. So yes, it's much shorter because pop songs are created for radio. Years ago, there was much experimentation and study put into what would work on radio as far as how long the song needed to be for the listener. This structure was designed to this length in part because it's an optimal duration that keeps the listener interested for the entire length of the song. Obviously, there are songs played on the radio that are longer and shorter, but this is the guide that most people follow.

The 32 bars are usually broken up into chunks of 8-measure (bar) sections. Below is the AABA format:

Verse 1

Verse 2

Bridge 1

Verse

Another standard format in pop music is the ABA structure. The A stands for the verse, and B stands for the chorus. Another reason it is important to study pop music is that although other genres' formats are a little different, they still build the structure from similar concepts and structures.

Chapter Review

Learning song structure is critical when it comes to DJ'ing, because you are going to need to know when the best time to start mixing the two tracks together is. Each genre follows a fairly specific song structure, and once you figure it out, most tracks will fall in line with that particular structure. The more you know about music theory and how songs are constructed, the better the DJ you will become because you will be able to assess which songs work together the best, based on what key they were created in.

Exercise

- Pick out three electronic music tracks. Count out how many bars are in the entire track of each, and also count out how many bars are in the chorus/hook sections. As previously stated, the number of bars in a track will vary, but most tracks in the main genres will feature a chorus/hook with 32 bars.

- Pick out three pop songs. Count out how many bars are in each entire song. Can you find the choruses? Where are the verses?

Developing Your Own Style

"A great DJ is someone who masters anything from vinyl, CDs to MIDI controllers and added drum machines/EFX, but who can blow a crowd away simply by using two 12x10s and a 2-channel mixer." —Martin Bundsen

Finding your style of music is key. Whether you want to become a world-famous DJ or just want to play for your friends at their house parties, it is important to develop your own philosophy as a DJ and give your audience a fun experience that they will remember. Are you going to be a techno, electro, trance, breaks, or hip-hop DJ? Of course, you can always cross over into many genres. Even though the kind of music you play has a lot to do with your unique style, that's certainly not all there is to it. For example, what kind of interaction will you have with the crowds you play for? Will you have a certain kind of outfit? A signature way you mix with regard to the way you move your body? If you want to be a great DJ, part of it will be the showmanship aspect of the craft. Obviously, you don't have to get into all of that if you don't want to, but if you want to entertain, creating theater can be a great thing. Have fun with it—your style is completely up to you.

My style was something that I grew into over time and it keeps evolving. Because I was a musician before I learned how to DJ, I wanted my DJ sets to feature my live percussion. It was also important for me to have crowd interaction and to move around onstage or in the DJ booth as much as possible. I enjoy high-energy experiences, and this was something I wanted to give to people at shows as well. My style and philosophy evolved. When I first started DJ'ing, I was concerned about what people thought about my performances. This is a good trait to have because, after all, an entertainer is there to entertain.

But on the flip side, if you focus too much on what other people think, you will lose your style—and you don't want that to happen. So I had to rein it in a bit. Once I did, I went a little too far with what I wanted sometimes, and for a short period, I simply didn't care what people thought. I was going to play what I wanted no matter how the crowd responded. Looking back on it, I was operating like this way back in 2009. I had gotten to a point of defining the kind of style that I loved, and I became inflexible about which tracks I played during a set. Most of the time, I was going to absolutely hammer a set with high-octane electro house tracks, and I didn't budge.

Even though my shows were still a success and fun for people to dance to, this was not a good way to go about choosing my tracks because so much of my philosophy was about how important it is to connect with the crowd, and it's hard to truly connect with them if they are being shut out in any way. I'm not at all saying don't play what you want. But if you are reading the crowd, you can still play the music you like while giving the dance floor what it wants. It's a balance. The music I play during my shows in San Francisco is different from the shows I play in Berlin. I still play EDM, but Berlin likes a little bit different style than San Francisco.

Today, I can happily say that I have found a balance between playing what I want and what I read that the crowd is into. I went from trying to please people too much to playing only what I wanted to now going with the flow and playing music that I know will create a great vibe on the dance floor. As I alluded to earlier, in 2009 I had gotten to a place where I was very decisive about what I would play. There is nothing wrong with that, per se, but I got to a point where I thought that electro house was the be-all and end-all when it came to EDM. This was funny, because I am someone who loves a wide range of EDM and music in general.

When I moved to Berlin, I again started going out to watch other DJs . . . something I had stopped doing. The result was that I was awakened to the fact that part of being a great DJ is the realization that it wasn't about me—that I am a conduit, whose purpose is to provide an amazing and fun experience for people on the dance floor. So staying true to what moves you as a DJ, while finding the balance of what your audience desires, is a fun challenge, and hopefully it'll evolve for you over time the way it has for me. It's a process you will hopefully go through as well.

As I've mentioned, different parts of the world are into different sounds, so it's important to take note and see which styles work best where you are performing. If you are playing shows mostly in the city where you live, a great way to find out what music is popular is to go out and see what is working in the clubs. When you are playing shows in cities and countries you don't live in, one way to find out is to ask the promoter what is hot right now. And as you become more familiar with the industry landscape, you will get a sense of which styles of music various countries gravitate toward. For example, right now dubstep and electro are massive in North America, but in Europe they aren't as big. Berlin has always been known for techno and genres that feature a deep and dark sound. Being a DJ is about educating yourself on what styles work well, and with a little digging and reading magazines like *DJ Mag* and *Mixmag*, it's pretty easy to figure out. Ultimately, though, I believe that if you are having fun while you DJ, that energy will be contagious and your dance floor will likely have fun as well.

If you appreciate a wide range of music like I do, this will give you an opportunity to expand your horizon as a DJ/artist. Even if you want to be known as a dubstep DJ/producer only, learning and listening to different styles will enhance your skill set as that kind of DJ because it'll give you a different perspective that you can take back into your genre of choice. This mentality is the very perspective that helps people pioneer new genres and ideas.

Try the exercise below:

- Set aside some time during the week and write for ten to fifteen minutes about your five favorite musical genres. This will give you an opportunity to get clear about which style or styles you are most passionate. Do these styles blend well together? Or are they completely different? If they are similar, you'll be able to DJ them together. If they are quite different, then you might have to develop a different DJ alias. For example, dubstep and trance don't really mix well together. But if you like both genres, when you are getting ready to choose a DJ name, you could choose one for the trance sets and one for the dubstep.

- It's never too soon to start thinking about a DJ name. I think that using your real name for at least one of your aliases is a good idea. For example, I use my name and also use the Banger Bros. The Banger Bros is all about electro, and my real name is more for my proper house and techno sets. Set aside time this week to write down and brainstorm some DJ names for yourself.

Mixing

One of the most important things about mixing that a DJ must learn is timing. You will want the track that you are mixing in to start at the beginning of a musical phrase, and both tracks need to be in time with one another. You also need to make sure that the two tracks are lined up perfectly so that when both are playing at the same time, the listener thinks that only one track is playing. The best DJs are the ones who can hold their mixes to the point that even a

DJ has a hard time figuring out if there are two tracks playing, or just one. To ensure that you have learned the building blocks of timing when you start mixing, it's simply about knowing a little song structure, as described in chapter 14, "Song Structure and Music Basics."

The basic principle of mixing is the art of beatmatching and blending two songs together while matching their tempo and keeping them in perfect synchronization. In an ideal world, your entire mix would sound like one long track.

Five Essential Keys to Mixing

- **Timing.** Stay true to the tip of mixing at the beginning of a musical phrase, and make sure that you mix your second track in time with the one that is already playing. Once you have the timing down, you need to be able to keep the tracks playing at the same speed. This is accomplished by using the pitch control function on your CDJ or turntable. Something to keep in mind here is the original tempo of each track you are mixing. For example, if one track's tempo is 125 and the other's is 124, you will know right away that you shouldn't have to perform drastic pitch control movements. Obviously, the further apart each track's original tempo is, the more adjustments and tweaks you'll need to make.

- **Levels.** It's essential to make sure that your volume levels are comparable; if you mix in the second track at a much higher volume, your mix is going to sound bad. The volumes of tracks vary because no music producer or mastering engineer mixes the same. Because of this, you will find that some tracks are louder than others, which is yet another reason why it's important to know the tracks you play. Volume discrepancy is easy to work with and adjust, if need be.

- **Mix placement.** It's important that you mix in your second track in a desirable place in your mix. As I've mentioned before, you typically want to have your second track introduced to the dance floor and out the main speakers when the first track has resolved its 32-bar phrase. And remember, most dance music is formatted in 32-bar chunks, so this is the standard. The best place to start mixing is at the beginning of a 32-bar section. You might have heard that if a teacher mentions something three times, then it's important and will probably be on the test. This is certainly the case with making sure that your mix placement is on point.

- **Beatmatching.** Timing, timing, timing. That's the key to beatmatching. Once you have aligned both tracks so they are playing in time, you will need to keep them playing at the same tempo. This is accomplished by adjusting your pitch control. If you did a good job with beatmatching, your adjustments will be minor. If one track is playing too fast, slow it down and vice versa. A quick tip for beatmatching is to gently push or grab the turntable platter. For example, if one track is playing too fast, gently grab the platter to pull it back in time with the track you are mixing it with. This is to get your tracks back in time when they drift off. From here, you'll need to readjust the pitch control to match the speeds of the respective tracks.

- **Crossfading.** A crossfade creates a transition from one song to the next. Like many techniques in DJ'ing there are no rules, merely guidelines to help you along your path. With the crossfader, you can create an abrupt transition by moving the fader quickly. If you want a smooth transition, just slide the crossfader slowly in the direction that you desire.

> **Important Note:** Remember, if the crossfader is all the way to one side, only one channel will be sending audio out through the main speakers. If it is in the middle, both channels are audible. Play around with the crossfader to see which method works better for you.

Exercise

A mantra I've remembered since I was a kid is Practice Makes Permanent. There's an old saying, "Practice makes perfect." My Dad was my soccer coach for a few years, and I remember after one of our practices he mentioned to us that practice makes permanent. His message was to make your practice as precise as possible, because the habits you form will have a lasting effect. With that in mind, your mantra as a budding DJ is that you can never have enough practice. Try the exercises below to help you practice some of the information you learned in this chapter:

- Work into your daily practice routine the tools in this chapter. Spend five minutes practicing a smooth crossfade transition, and then spend another five with the abrupt approach.

- Put an extra emphasis on using your overall tempo function to control the tempo of your tracks, especially on CDJs. Remember when I mentioned that if you are adjusting only the jog wheel, your tracks will go out of time? This is because your overall tempo function is the one that controls how fast or slow your track is going. Adjusting this function is the best way to adjust the tracks.

Sets and Shows

Selecting music is a skill and one of the essential elements in creating an entertaining show. If you hear people talk about how a DJ is good at programming his or her sets, this is what they are referring to. When you go watch a DJ play, you know he is playing a good show if everybody is dancing and having a good time. A big reason for this is because the DJ knows her crowd and is playing music that she knows will get them on the dance floor. If a DJ is not great at mixing but is good at selecting tracks that the crowd loves, a lot of people will let it slide if there is a train wreck happening on every mix. I'm not saying that you should drive to excel at programming and forget about mixing, but if all you were to do was select great tracks, you'll at least get the crowd moving. I bring this up to illustrate the point that the process of becoming a great DJ takes time. So if you are good at something like programming, then you might be ready to DJ at a club sooner than you think. Perfectionism be gone! Have you ever seen a DJ who was just not able to get people dancing? They are not aware of the kind of music their crowd likes. We have all seen shows like that. In fact, I have been that DJ who plays the wrong style of music to a crowd. Thankfully, those moments were few and far between and don't happen anymore.

So your music selection is key. Whether it's hip-hop or dance music, know your crowd and give them what they want. Previously, I stated that it's important to stay true to your sound, so don't think that I am saying that you should move away from that. During my sets and shows, I DJ only EDM. When I mentioned I wasn't playing the kind of music my crowd enjoyed, it's not like I was playing electro house and they wanted to two-step to country music. Nope, not at all. It was simply a case in which I was either not playing the most danceable tracks in a specific genre or playing electro but the crowd wanted techno. Fixing that problem was simple, and it's always a balance of playing exactly what you want to play with regard to what will work best for that particular crowd. Eventually, you'll only want to play the type of shows where you enjoy the kind of music that the promoter brings to the nightclub. For example, there is a promoter friend of mine in the south of Russia who produces events that are geared mostly toward pop-style dance music. Even though I like playing music that is a little more underground, I also enjoy pop/dance music as well. So, even though that style is not my favorite, it's one of them. See the point? I'm still playing what I want; it's simply down the spectrum from what I like most.

> **Quick Tip:** People like to hear what's familiar to them, so if you want to introduce new music with the best results, the most effective way to accomplish this is by playing a track that you think most people in the club will recognize, and then follow it up with a new track you discovered. For example, if you are DJ'ing for a Top 40 or dance/pop crowd and want to introduce an underground track, first play that remix of a tune everybody knows. Then drop your hidden gem. Same goes for any other environment. If you are playing for an underground party and want to introduce a track you just got that nobody has heard yet, play a well-known tune in the genre you are spinning at the moment.

As far as selecting your setlist, there are a couple of philosophies about this. Some DJs like to have their set 100 percent prepared before they play—everything from genre to order to song title. This is similar to how some bands might prepare for a set, in that it's preprogrammed. I used to use this same method. Leading up to the event, I would start to pick out tracks I might want to play. Then the night before a show, I would think about what kind of crowd I would be performing for and would go through my collection, picking out my favorite tracks in that specific genre. It was a great way for me to relieve some of my stress during the show, because I had already picked everything out. Since then, though, I have changed my philosophy and have modified how I approach each show. I still spend quite a bit of prep time, perhaps even more than when I was starting out. But some of my prep might surprise you, as I spend a lot of time visualizing the show being a success. This is a great tool, especially because instead of preprogramming my sets, I prefer to let the energy of the particular show dictate what I will play. I still go through my collection and pick out a couple of new promos for the show, but I am doing this only to get a gist of what I might play. For example, if I am playing a show at an underground club in Europe, I'll go through my tech house, techno, and house tracks. If I'm playing a show in Seattle, I'll dig into electro. Something to keep in mind when playing a show, especially when you are starting out, is to make sure that you are playing songs you are comfortable mixing. Don't purchase a bunch of new tracks the night before a show. I know it's exciting to get new music, but it's more important that you are confident during your show. Mixing songs that you are familiar with will help with that. Bring along a couple of new ones to introduce, but not an entire set!

As much as I've tweaked and refined with my sets and sounds, I of course have developed my sound, so people will not hear certain types of music during my shows and come to expect at least a similar vibe. But I don't pick the order the night before; I show up to the show with my best tunes, and simply go with the flow. The most important thing to remember is to play songs that you like and know other people will appreciate. The crowd will feed off of your energy. Knowing your tracks inside out is another key.

Story

Having a bad set happens to even the best of us. A bad set can come in a few different forms. One example is when either most of your crowd is not dancing and/or you "train" wreck your mixes. A train wreck is when your mixes are so off time that it sounds like a train jolted off the tracks and crashed into the mountain! Another is if you are in a bad mood and are not able to be present with your audience because you are thinking about how upset you are. Whatever you have going on in your life, it's important that you leave that out of your set and focus on having a good time. This shouldn't be a problem, as DJ'ing tends to demand your full attention and is therapeutic as well.

I have experienced bad sets that created disharmonious moods, both as a member of the audience and as the DJ. I remember a particular set I was playing in Seattle that wasn't necessarily a bad set, but at the beginning of my set, the previous DJ was angry about something and he and I got into an argument. I kept my head, but it was a bit uncomfortable. By the time I went onstage I was upset, and the first song that I played was the wrong song to play and created a negative vibe in the club. People were still dancing, but I could feel the negativity in the club. On top of that, there was an extremely drunk guy in the DJ booth who constantly kept touching me and trying to talk to me while I was mixing. Needless to say, the first few minutes were a struggle until someone form Security removed him. Fortunately, I was able to right the ship and did my best to stay focused on mixing, despite the belligerent guy in the DJ booth.

But the lesson here is that as a DJ we all have to learn how to deal with situations outside of our control. It's a wild atmosphere, and sometimes things go haywire. It can get crazy in a club, and if someone gets angry, don't take it personally. Just deal with whatever situation comes your way by keeping your cool, if you can. Below are some strategies for building your sets.

Setlist Strategies

- Even though I started off preprogramming my sets before a show, I strongly recommend that you simply bring your favorite tracks to the show and play them in an undetermined order. The vibe of the dance floor will guide you. Just completely go with the flow!

- Another important element to a successful set is how you build you energy. You are going to be taking your crowd on a musical journey. Some DJs like to build their set slowly, so they might start off with songs that are lower energy. The philosophy here is to warm up the crowd and then once the room is filled and everybody is dancing, you play your most exciting music. Think of it like an airplane taking off. Again, feel free to experiment with this, because rules are made to be broken. I used to come out of the gate with guns blazin'. Right from the word "go," the energy was extremely high. But there's one problem with going this route. What happens if you play your most high-energy track first? Only place to go is down, right? This is not to say that it's still not a good idea to come out firing right away.

- A different approach is to spike your set in chunks. Sometimes I like to start a set off with a bang and in the middle of it play sets that are more laid back. Once I near the end, I bring that energy up to a crescendo. Keep in mind, my sets are usually all very high energy, so when I am playing a "laid back" tune, its energy would be considered high for most people. Experimenting with the ways you organize the energy flow can be fun. Make sure you pay attention to the various reactions each variation receives. This way you'll be able to make adjustments for what works best. Keep in mind that the way you organize the flow of your set will also be affected by which time slot you play in. If you are opening up the entire night, you will be better served to start off more chilled out. If you are playing the peak-hour set, this is where more experimentation is in order.

- The night before a show, think about the kind of crowd you might be playing for. If they are a dance music crowd, do they like electro, techno, or trance, funky house, dubstep? Is it an underground crowd, or do they like mainstream music? Once you have determined the kind of crowd, go through your collection and pick out songs accordingly. If you are not going to predetermine your set, then picking out tracks in your collection the night before can serve as a guideline for the type of style and tracks that you might be playing during the show. It's also useful to organize your songs in your library or CD or record case by style or genre. This way when you're flipping through what track to play next at the show, you have a basic idea of where to find what you are looking for.

The Wedding or Graduation Setlist

Playing at a wedding is going to be different than playing at a graduation party. And playing at a club or festival is going to be different than both of those as well.

I have never played at a wedding or graduation party, but I know that if you are DJ'ing for a wedding, the bride and groom are going to give you a playlist and you are going to have to play what they want you to play. I know DJs who do a lot of weddings and say it can be a lot of fun. One friend in particular is a local and well-known San Francisco DJ, so a lot of times the weddings he gets asked to play at are given by people who love EDM and the vibes can be pretty funky and fun. Some wedding DJs make decent money, so if you don't mind working from a playlist given to you by the bride and groom, you might want to try it out to see if you like it.

At graduations and private parties, the setlist will be simple. Which artists are popular with your classmates? Play all the favorites mixed in with a little bit of your own flavor. DJ'ing for a private party can actually be a lot of fun. It's not always the way it happens, but in many cases the people who hire you for such an event might have seen your set at a nightclub. I've done several private parties in this circumstance, and the people hiring me just wanted me to do what I do. I highly recommend doing some private parties, because in the right setting, they are intimate and fun.

Fashion Shows

DJ'ing for a fashion show is a mixture between doing a private party and a wedding in that the designer and/or people hiring you for the event will probably have a particular vibe they have in mind. But they might also know about the style of music you play and, depending on the situation, might give you the liberty to DJ what you'd like . . . within the context of the vibe they want to create. It really all depends on the situation, though. Many times the entire setlist is worked out in advance, and they just want you to play what they give you at exactly the right moment as it pertains to the show. I've done a couple of fashion shows, and they are certainly an experience worth checking out.

Practice Schedule

Having a practice schedule is another one of the keys to becoming a great DJ and artist. Over time, my practice schedule has changed. Below are outlines of practice schedules when I first started out and my present schedule. Along with actually physically practicing, what many people don't realize is that visualization also counts for practice. I highly recommend doing as much of both as possible.

Starting Out

At the same time I was in school for music, percussion and sound production, I was also working at a gym in Minneapolis and managing a property. I practiced music production for about two hours per night, drums for thirty minutes per day, and DJ'ing for one hour a night. After I was finished with my schooling, my practice shifted a bit. I was now DJ'ing for one to two hours per night, practicing percussion for one hour per night, and doing gigs on the weekend. At the time, I was in an African drum group, traveling around the West Coast and performing with two Grammy Award–winning percussionists.

Chapter Review

As you embark along your journey as a DJ, it's likely that you will experiment a lot with regard to whether you pre-program your sets and where you play certain tracks in your set. It's critical that you pay attention to the timing of your set and the vibe of the crowd. If you have time to build a set, I recommend taking the crowd on that journey. If your set is short and there are a lot of people on the dance floor, feel free to come out of the gate with high energy. Experiment and have fun—you'll find what works best for you and your crowds.

If you are going to DJ for weddings, fashions shows, or private parties, just realize that in many cases you'll be playing music that someone else wants you to play. In these situations you become a bit of a request machine. There's nothing wrong with this, just something to keep in mind as you are figuring out which types of DJ situations you want to get into.

Exercise

Even though eventually you probably won't be preprograming your sets, the following exercise will give the opportunity to develop the feel of an entire set.

- Design a one-hour set for a show if you were the opening DJ at your favorite club in your city. Keep in mind that since you are opening up the night, the energy of your set will be more laid back than if you were playing the main slot. There is a reason that this spot is often called the "warm-up" set/slot. If the club is fairly empty, you'll want to start off mellow and build up the energy from there.

- Now design a one-hour set as if you were playing the headlining slot. Are you starting off with a bang? Or are you building to a crescendo? Remember, if the dance floor is full, you can feel free to start off your set with high energy.

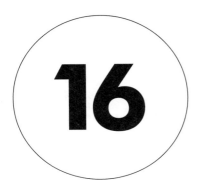

Adding Live Instruments

> "If you are able to connect your passion for music with your heart, you become a great DJ." —EDX

Let's talk about adding your instrument into the mix. Here is where things are going to get even more exciting. As you become comfortable with mixing, it's now time to play your instrument during your set.

I believe that technological advances have a mostly positive impact on our society. The music industry is no different and has been greatly affected by technology, and I'm all for it. Some people think that technology is killing the art and craft of DJ'ing, but I disagree and feel it is providing a window of opportunity for artists to actually mix technology with the organic nature of live performance. As most DJs switch toward a computer-based mixing system, the easier it becomes for DJs to do other things while they mix. Imagine you are at a show and the DJ is spending most of his set with his head buried in their computer. Maybe once in a while he throws his hands up or gets into it. Kinda boring, don't you think? Now imagine a DJ onstage who is playing a guitar while she mixes, or maybe she is playing with an entourage of synthesizers and percussion instruments. Much more interesting, isn't it? People in today's DJ culture are clamoring for artists to get back to the roots of live performance, even if it's an add-on to the set, rather than being a full band or ensemble. You see, music fans have to deal with what we provide for them. So it's up to you to create something special, and adding live performance to your set is an amazing way to do this.

As you introduce your instrument into your shows, you are not only creating something unique and exciting, but you are also instantly setting yourself apart from the crowd of DJs in the industry. From my experience the instruments that work the best with a DJ set are those where the crowd can see that you are doing something. Live percussion is great because you will be moving your hands and arms quite a bit, so it's easy for the crowd to see you are doing something back there. A sax is another great instrument. Keyboards work well, but because you'd likely be using a digital controller, it's sometimes difficult for the crowd to realize you are doing anything other than mixing because the sounds blend a bit too much with the music. I'm not saying it doesn't work—I just remember people saying to us after our shows that they didn't know we were using keyboards, but that they could tell instantly when we were playing percussion. In my opinion, you can experiment with using live instruments in most situations when it comes to DJ'ing. But keep in mind that a sax is a lead instrument, so make sure to play it during places in a track that won't compete with the lead instruments. Whatever you choose to play, you'll want to create a space where all of the instruments and elements are working together. Practice this daily at home, as this is a craft that will take some time to perfect. Every time you do a show where you are playing your live instrument, people will remember you. You will be creating something authentic, something that captivates the crowd and emits passion. They might not remember your name at first, but when they talk about your set, they will say, "Hey do you remember that DJ playing the guitar during that set on Saturday night? That was awesome!"

Don't worry about being perfect in the beginning. Since you are going to be DJ'ing while playing an instrument at the same time, it's going to take some experimentation and a lot of practice to make it all work. To this day, I am still refining the way I incorporate my African drum. The challenge is always to play the drum as much as possible while still maintaining a fluid mixing flow. Something I believe that helped me is that I started playing my drums along to my set right when I was learning how to DJ. Needless to say, I had growing pains along the way! With that being said, on the rare occasion that I DJ without playing percussion, I feel like something is missing. But again, don't take things too seriously here . . . have fun with it—after all, that is what it's all about. The more comfortable you are, the easier and more seamless the act will be.

Story

When I was learning how to DJ, I didn't wait long before I tested my new skills at a club. Looking back on it, I don't regret my approach of taking action before I had perfected my skills, because my ability to get in there and make things happen has gotten me where I am now. If you wait until everything is perfect, you'll miss out on a mountain of opportunities. I definitely logged plenty of error-filled performances that cost me losing dance floors! But overall, the experiences were mostly positive and provided learning experiences that can be gained only when you get behind the booth, or onstage. If you are willing to put yourself out there quickly, just be prepared to face some potential criticism. Some of my fellow DJ friends tell me that they practiced in their basement for years before they took they felt comfortable enough to play in front of a crowd. If you do this, that's fine, too. It's a recommended approach taken by many, but I have never done anything thing this way. I firmly believe in the philosophy of pushing your limits. Taking positive risks is one of the best ways for one to go beyond what you think is possible. I recommend that you at least know that you have a fairly strong grasp on DJ'ing before you get yourself out there. Be smart about it; you will know when you are ready to play in front of others. The sooner the better!

So how do you blend it all together? When is the best time to play your instrument, and how often should you play? In my experience, there are two major points during the mixing process when you can add in your improvisation: playing along with one track in the mix or playing along with two. How often you should play? I think the more you can play, the better! The best place to play your live instrument is during the main sections because you'll have a nice 32-bar chunk of time to riff along to. Obviously, you won't be able to play for the entire duration of it because you'll need to get ready to mix the next track. But this is the time to incorporate your instrument, because it will give you the most time to play along. This is easier said than done, but the more practice you get both with DJ'ing and playing an instrument while DJ'ing, the easier it will be for you to extend your instrument playing during your sets.

Playing Along with One Track in the Mix

Yes, it's pretty self-explanatory and is as basic as it sounds. This method is the simplest because you don't have to worry about holding your mix since the audience will only hear one song. During this method you can pick any section in the song that you are inspired to play along with. Since you are literally not mixing at all here, you can relax—it's all about riffing away, instead of listening closely to if your mix is solid while also playing instruments. It's much easier to play your live instrument while only one track is playing in the mix. If you play an instrument while you are mixing two of your tracks together, you have to make sure your tracks stay in time, while also playing your instrument. That's a lot to account for!

Although this is the easier method, remember that you still have to select your next track to play and begin the next mix. Even though this is the easiest of the methods, you will have to give yourself plenty of time so you keep the dance floor moving without stopping the music. What do I mean by that? What if you are playing along to the track, and suddenly it ends?! Silence is a dance floor killer, so you don't want that to happen. Part of the art of playing with an instrument is not only finding the right places in the mix to play but also being able to find the next track without it affecting your playing.

Playing Along with Two Tracks

This is the most difficult to master, because now you have two tracks playing in the mix while you are playing your instrument. This method requires more of your attention in making sure that everything is lined up in the mix and that you are playing in time with everything. There's a lot to account for, with a lot of "moving parts"! If the songs are not precisely synced, they will drift off-tempo, so you will need to make sure your tracks stay aligned while you are riffing away on your instrument. For example, if you are in the middle of a ripping solo on the keys and hear that one track is drifting away from the tempo of the other track, you have to quickly go back to DJ'ing and make sure to get everything aligned again. Not an easy task, to say the least, but you will get it down before you know it. Adjusting on the fly is part of the process. Something to keep in mind if you are one of the DJs who plan on strictly mixing on the computer: this process of playing a live instrument is much simpler on a computer-based mixing system because the tracks you mix tend to stay in time due to the sync-mixing function. This is why I mentioned that computer-based mixing opens up a whole new world of possibilities for live instrumentation.

Another one of the challenges of playing an instrument during a mix is the amount of time that you will actually be playing it. A lot of your time is going to be spent making sure that your mix is running smoothly, and finding the next track can take a while. In bands or any other "live" outfit, you are spending the entire time playing your instrument. But when doing this in your DJ set, you will now have two instruments dividing your time: your instrument of choice and the turntables. If one is neglected, you might as well just be doing one or the other. The one that usually gets neglected is your instrument. But not to worry, you'll simply just need to remind yourself to work it into the mix by playing it.

Switching between your mixer and your instrument means less time with one of them, so it's all about making sure that you are extrafocused. The instrument you choose to play will naturally receive less time than the turntables. Because of this, it will be up to you to give your instrument as much attention as possible. Experiment with how long you can play your instrument while managing the flow of your set. This is multitask heaven at its best, or a nightmare, depending on your perspective.

My favorite thing to do these days is to mix two tracks while playing my African percussion. It's a lot of fun to have three things going at once and oftentimes the climax of a tune happens when both records are playing at the same time, so adding my percussion accentuates the intensity. It didn't happen overnight that I was able to do this comfortably, and as I've mentioned, the biggest challenge is playing your instrument as long and as frequently as possible. To maximize the amount that you are able to play the live instrument, make sure that you start playing it as quickly as possible. For example, say you'd like to try method number one. The instant you've successfully mixed the track in that you are playing next, grab your instrument and start shredding away. Remember that you will want to start mixing your next track in at the beginning of a 32-bar phrase. So this gives you some time to play, while thinking about which track you will mix in next. Again, there's a lot to think about and to account for, but the more you do it, the more comfortable you will be.

Tips for Playing in the Mix

Focus on where and when the best times to play your live instrument in the mix. Mastering these aspects is key to a great performance.

Method 1

Once you have only one track playing, break out your instrument and play along. You might want to consider preprogramming your sets at first so that you can practice where you are going to play live in the mix. As I mentioned earlier, I don't preprogram my sets anymore, because doing so takes away the fun of reading the crowd. But I did when I started. So for the sake of keeping things simple, preprogram all of your sets at first. This will allow you to eliminate the time it takes to select your next track and enable you to focus on mixing and playing your instrument, which is already plenty to handle. Any time you can save will allow you to play your live instrument that much more. At the beginning, this will be extremely helpful with regard to maximizing the amount of time you play live. Once you start to get more comfortable, do away with programming your sets.

If you don't want to preprogram your sets, that's okay too. Although I recommend it at first, just make sure that your tracks are organized so you don't waste time searching for the next track instead of playing your instrument. A great way to do this is by simply organizing tracks by genre. If you are DJ'ing with CDJs, then you can make sure the CDs of each genre are next to each other in the case. If you are DJ'ing with a software program, then you can simply create folders of each of the genres. For example, you could create a folder for your dubstep tracks, your electro tracks, techno, tech house, and so on. The less time you spend searching for the next track to mix, the more time you'll have to play the instrument. Sometimes I played shows early on where I was so focused on making the mix solid that I did not play my drum as much. It's not that I didn't want to play my drum more; I was just concerned with making sure I didn't train wreck my mixes.

Something else to keep in mind if you don't want to preprogram your sets is to just map out the songs you will play back-to-back in the places you will incorporate your instrument. This way you can still go with the flow for most of your set, while ensuring that you are solid in the places when you will be both mixing and playing the instrument.

One of the biggest challenges of playing your live instrument while you DJ is being able to play it long enough, giving the crowd a proper dose of live instrumentation. I remember friends coming up to me after a show and asking why I didn't play more percussion. My brother was the person who would criticize me the most for this. At the time, it really was frustrating to hear him say he wished I would play my drum more, but it was extremely helpful feedback because it motivated me to work on playing the drum for longer periods of time during my shows. It's possible that this will happen for you as well, so strive to play your instrument for longer periods during your sets. Ask your friends for feedback. For example, ask them if they thought you played your instrument enough during your set. When you are able to get to the point of playing for longer periods of time, your crowd will thank you for it.

Method 2

As mentioned, this is a bit harder to pull off, but when you can nail it, it's a lot of fun and very rewarding! You can also play your instrument while you have both of your tracks playing at once. The risk and reward here is high because the potential for things going wrong is much higher. If, for example, you are playing your instrument and your tracks go out of time, then you'll have a train wreck on your hands. I recommend getting good at method 1 before trying method 2 out at a show. Both techniques are important to practice, but method 2 takes more time to develop. Becoming the ultimate DJ is about mastering the essentials of the DJ'ing craft, but it also means going beyond what most people expect. It's all about putting in something extra; that's what greatness is made of. Besides, if you are a DJ who is playing a live instrument while you DJ, it will be hard for someone to complain that you are not musical, because in fact you are a musician. Whenever I hear a musician complain that DJs are not musicians, I know that they are not talking about me. That could be the case for you as well.

Chapter Review

Playing a live instrument while DJ'ing is rewarding, fun, and unique. It's also a skill that takes time and effort to perfect. Your big challenge will be to make sure that you are playing your live instrument as much as possible while you DJ. Make sure to remind yourself to play it during your sets as much as you can.

Organizing your tracks is a big part of making your job easier when playing a live instrument while you DJ. You don't want to be searching for too long to find the next track, because that will take you away from valuable live instrumentation time.

Exercise

Using the techniques illustrated in this chapter, carve out some time during your daily practice to incorporate playing your live instrument in the mix. Remember, this can be any instrument you'd like to try.

1. Practice method 1.

2. Then practice method 2.

What were some of the challenges with each? How can you make the process smoother?

Stage Presence

Another important piece to becoming among the best of the best is cultivating excellent stage presence. How many times have you watched a DJ at a show who doesn't look as though he or she is excited about what they are doing? Way too many, right?! Having an energetic stage presence makes a world of difference. The best shows I have experienced are those in which the performer projected enthusiastic energy, interacted with the crowd, and looked like they were having fun up there. I can still remember the first time I saw Donald Glaude, one of the most famous DJs in America, perform in Seattle. Even as he strutted up to the DJ booth, you could tell he was about to drop a rockin' set. He was so pumped up and the crowd fed off of it; it was amazing. Every move he made exuded confidence, and his smile filled up the room. Who doesn't want to be around someone having a good time? At that moment, I knew I wanted to be a performer like that.

Stage presence is an often overlooked and underappreciated aspect of being an artist, but it's critical if you want to be among the best of the best. Although it is not talked about as a specific skill, it is one of the important factors that separate the extraordinary DJ from an average or good one. DJ'ing in front of a crowd is absolutely a live performance. If you are just going to stand up there twisting knobs with your head down, you might as well stay in your bedroom. The music industry is about entertainment, so the more ways you can engage the crowd, the more fun you'll have in the process and the better the performance it will be. Why is that? Because it's all about connecting with people. Music brings us together, and if you exude fantastic stage presence, you will enhance your ability to facilitate that.

When I was auditioning to perform with the Drum Café, an African percussion ensemble that performs interactive team building shows for corporations around the world, the owner gave me a valuable tip. He told me that since there are often thousands of people in attendance at a performance, I must project big energy onstage in order to be successful in his group. He suggested I take a course in theater performance, so I could learn to exude magnetic energy. Although I didn't take theater classes, I happened to be in a self-development course at the time, which was teaching us how to speak in front of large crowds. The class taught me not only how to be comfortable onstage but also how to significantly create and project the ability to exude "big" energy. I highly recommend you look into developing this energy as one of your tools. Whether you participate in a theater course or one on public speaking, it will prove invaluable for your live performances.

One of the most helpful tips I got in a class I took was that our nervousness is going to be there and that we can use it to help generate more energy. I still get nervous before shows, and I'm glad I do because it just means that I'm excited and, indeed, alive. However, the more we play shows, that nervousness is replaced by more of an excitement. I'm not saying it totally goes away, but it's more manageable and it doesn't feel as scary as it feels when first starting out. It's also helpful to remember to project a big energy and to embrace your nervousness . . . it's a human emotion. But if nervous energy is not dealt with properly, it can get out of hand and can work against you.

Here are two ways to ensure that you keep it in check. First, the more you prepare for your show, both by using the visualization technique I mentioned and going through the tracks you'll possibly play, the more comfortable you'll feel when the lights go on. The second way is to breathe and meditate before your set. It sounds simple, but when we get nervous, we don't breathe as much as we should. So set five minutes aside before the show and slow your mind down by taking deep breaths. Also, think about something that soothes you. If you make sure to practice these techniques leading up to your sets, your shows will go much more smoothly. And remember, when you are visualizing during the week, visualize people coming up to you after your show saying how great the set was. And what if you visualize your performance being a success but you totally bomb it? The reality of the situation is that we are still human and you are not perfect.

Visualization is a powerful tool, but it doesn't ensure that every set is going to be perfect. But there is research illustrating that people who visualize being successful are in fact more often successful than those who don't. There is a reason that Olympic and pro athletes spend a lot of their time visualizing themselves succeed. There are also researchers who say that one hour of visualization is equal to eight hours of practice time. In my experience, I perform much better when I visualize. The difference between doing it and not is night and day, actually. And as I mentioned earlier, when I was playing baseball, I was at my best when I visualized. Did that mean I was perfect? Absolutely not! Visualization will help you create more success as a DJ. If your performance doesn't match the success of the way you visualized it, don't worry—it will in time. When I am performing, it's important to me that I accomplish two things during a show. One is to, of course, have fun. If something is not fun, then what's the point? And two, is to make sure that I connect with the crowd, and that they are also having fun. And how does one connect with the crowd? It's very simple. Being present during your set is a major piece of it. All you need to do is give people in the audience eye contact, smile at them, and if you want to take it as far as I do, then you are going to have to cut the music for a split second and yell out to them, "Make some noise!" Or ask them how they are feeling. Depending on the size of the crowd, you might need a mic so they can hear you. Oftentimes, I throw in an expletive, but it's not necessary. For example, I say, "Make some f****** noise!" This lets them know that you have a pulse and are alive and kicking up there.

Why is it important to connect with the audience? Imagine that you are playing in front of eight thousand screaming fans. All of them are there for you and love your music. What if none of them showed up to the show? Well, that would mean you would not be playing that big show and instead would be playing in your basement for nobody, wouldn't it? Connecting with the crowd accomplishes a few things. First, it lets people know that you appreciate them, and second, it is fun to interact with your audience. Music is a celebration, and a performance is something that should bring people together. Since you are the one providing the vibe of the night, it's your responsibility to do this. It's a big responsibility, but it's also very simple. Just share your passion with them.

You have the potential to give people a good experience, so make it count. Whether I am performing in front of thousands of people or just five, I always make it my intention to connect with my audience. Without them, we have no stage, so it's my way of expressing gratitude to them.

Quick Tip: A great way to begin to project bigger energy is to practice yelling more. Now, obviously I'm not talking about yelling *at* someone. No, I am talking about like when you are in the car or somewhere private, where you can yell without someone thinking you are yelling at them. Once you find this place, practice yelling. When you first start doing this, it will sound like you are angry. That's not necessarily a bad thing, but as you practice, try not to sound so angry and just focus on projecting a loud voice. Just focus on projecting a loud voice and pay attention to your tone. The idea here is to project a strong voice. This is a great way to get used to projecting big energy. And as a bonus, if you feel comfortable enough, practice making big movements with your hands, making each gesture decisive and big. Because when you are onstage, the people who are not as close to you won't be able to see your movements unless they are big. It might feel weird practicing these two techniques, but sometimes the things that feel uncomfortable at first are the things that really help carry your work to another level. This is true for both of these tools.

Chapter Review

Are you going to show the crowd you are alive behind the decks and onstage? Are you going to interact with them and be engaging? Can you project an energy onstage that creates a positive vibe? We DJ because it's about sharing the love, and the better and more engaging your stage presence is, the more you will be aligned with the authentic nature of what it means to be a great DJ. Having great stage presence is about letting go of any restriction with your self-expression. Let the crowd know you are having fun doing what you do. Sometimes we live life trapped in a rubber suit. Cultivating stage presence is all about taking off the restrictions that come with wearing a rubber suit.

Exercise

This exercise is going to be a mixture of doing some research and taking some action that will help transform your energy onstage.

- Research your favorite DJs and find performances of theirs on YouTube. It's likely that you'll be drawn to a particular kind of stage presence and energy. For example, I am always drawn to DJs and performers with high energy who interact with the crowd. Whatever your taste, find that vibe and look at the kind of gestures they create during a set.

- If you live in a place where you drive your car often, then this exercise will be simpler for you to do. Even if you live in a place where driving is not the norm, find a place where you can be as loud as you want without having to worry about getting in trouble. Once you've sorted out your location, take two to three minutes and yell at the top of your lungs, while also making big and decisive gestures. You can even do this while singing along to the song; it doesn't matter how you project the energy—just make sure it's loud and big. Do this exercise for the week, but I highly recommend doing it whenever possible, as it will help you achieve a big and animated stage presence.

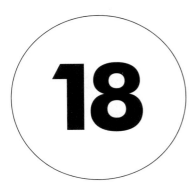

Reading Crowds

Paying attention to how your crowd is reacting to the tracks you are playing is absolutely essential. Why? If you are overly focused on mixing, going from one mix to the next without looking up, you'll have no idea if people are leaving the dance floor or not. Just because you dig a song doesn't mean that they will. And even if they like your track selections, it doesn't mean they'll be dancing. So do yourself a huge favor and check in with your dance floor.

There are always going to be people leaving the dance floor, whether it's to go to the bar or the toilet. As long as most of the crowd is dancing, then you'll know you are on the right track. If not, then you'll have to tweak your track selection. The only way to notice this is to check out the dance floor to see what's happening. At first this is sometimes difficult, because if you are new to DJ'ing, your focus will be on making sure you are beatmatching and mixing correctly. Of course, that is important, as you don't want to cause a train wreck every mix. But it's important to get into the habit of reading your crowd, because if nobody is dancing, who cares if your mixes are spot-on? I'm not saying not to worry about creating tight mixes, but those will come. The most important thing is whether the people on the dance floor are dancing.

If you notice your dance floor is thinning out, a great way to get back the crowd's attention is to play a remix or cover of a song that you think they will love. There's a reason that bands play cover songs. Most of the time when a band plays a popular cover song it's going to ignite the crowd. Many artists launch their careers by creating a cool cover of a popular classic. DJ'ing a cover song that is suitable for dance floors has a similar effect on your audience in that it often pulls them back onto the dance floor. Playing a popular remix or mashup achieves the same thing. I have a bootleg remix of the Guns N' Roses song "Welcome to the Jungle." This is one of my secret weapons, and almost always sends the crowd, no matter what country I'm performing in, into a frenzy.

If I'm losing the dance floor, all I have to do is drop this track and I'm back in business. I have other tracks like this, which I know will work in just about any situation. The key is to find secret weapons like this that will get your dance floor going. Sometimes it takes a lot of digging and looking for them, but once you find these, it'll be worth it. They can be great safety valves. The more you learn about the particular scene you are in, the more you are going to figure out what people like. For example, that Guns N' Roses bootleg remix generally works for electro crowds. It might work for a group that mostly is into techno, but I haven't tested that one out yet.

Chapter Review

It's important to see how the crowd reacts to what you play. If you are doing well, there will be a lot of people dancing. If there aren't, you've got to go in a different direction. One of the mistakes I made early on in my DJ career was that I was stubborn about what I played. Learning to be flexible in what I play is one of the things that have helped make my DJ sets more enjoyable.

Exercise

No matter where you live there should be at least some DJ shows and sets happening fairly close to your zip code. The more DJs you see perform live, the more you will learn about some of the things that separate the good DJs from the not so good. If you are old enough to get into twenty-one and over clubs, you will have more opportunities to see performances. If you are underage, you will not have access to as many, but no matter how old you are, there should be plenty of shows for you to check out. The more you attend, the better.

Each week, pick an event to attend. At the end of the night, take some notes on what you thought worked and what you thought needed improvement. Did the DJ ever lose the floor? Was there energy great? If you have a smart phone that has a notepad in it, you could even write notes during the show.

Part III

The Business

Marketing

Your brand and marketing are essential elements to your success. If you have something great to offer, the more people who know about you, the more opportunities you will have in securing more shows in more cities around the world. It's simply not enough to be an amazing talent. The most successful people in any profession are great at marketing themselves. Whether you do the marketing yourself or work with a team, spreading the word about what you do is essential. Having a great publicist can help you achieve great visibility. Publicists will make sure that your brand and music is visible in magazines, and they will make sure that you have interviews and that you are properly promoted.

Not every publicist or PR agency is created equal, so you will want to make sure to do some homework. I've worked with a number of publicists over the years, and the best ones are those who are responsive and reliable. A lot of publicists will promise you all kinds of publicity, but they don't come through with half of what they say they will. I would rather a publicist speak modestly about what they do. And I've found that these people usually come through with more than what they said they would and are also more reliable. When searching for a publicist, don't simply see who they've worked for, but get in touch with those people and ask what their experience was in working with that publicist or agency. Some might not get back to you, but others will. Most of all, though, pay attention to a couple of things: Are they delivering what they said they would? Are they reliable and responsive to your needs? If not, you might want to move on. But publicists are expensive, so if you don't have enough money to hire one, don't worry because you can be your own publicist until you have a positive cash flow.

When you do get to the point of needing a good publicist, I recommend Publicity Lab in the Netherlands (www.publicity-lab.com). Nicole Hofman has a great reputation, works with some of the biggest names in DJ'ing, is a great person, and is responsive to the needs of the artists she works with. I know this, because I have worked with her. And who says you can't be your own publicist? Before I had the money to spend on one, guess who was our publicist for CyberSutra, aka the Banger Bros? Yep, me. Nobody will work harder for your career than you will, and so if you are unable to hire someone, there is no better person than yourself to get your name out there. At the beginning you can write your own press releases and e-mail them editors of magazines in your genre. Something I learned just a few years ago is that most of the time, it's not a case of magazine writers tracking down managers of bands and artists they want to feature, but instead, it is either the publicist, the manager, or yes, *you* who is responsible for the content finding its way into a magazine. So brush up on your writing skills, send out your material to magazines, and get publicity. There is an accepted format that magazines use when choosing content, and you want to make sure to follow it so your mail will actually be read.

The below illustration is an example of a press release format that you can send out to magazines.

For Immediate Release

Rising star Scott Binder and Australia's heralded songstress Blue MC team up to create a dance floor smash, "Freedom." Weaving the sample from Tom Novy's "SuperStar," the dynamic duo creates a funky disco house tune that has a wide appeal for electronic music lovers.

Both Scott and Blue come from popular electronic music acts based in the United States and Australia, respectively. The two recently decided to also launch solo projects, linking up to create a few songs together and building a tour around an excited vibe that they are creating.

"Freedom" features a stellar remix package that includes mixes by one of the best electro house producers on the planet, Chrizz Luvly; the Banger Bros; the SpekrFreks; tech duo Rayner & Wisqo; JK Soul; and funk specialist Aldo Vanucci. The release covers a spectrum of sound that is already filling dance floors around the world.

Contact:

Nicole Hofman

info@publicity-lab.com

www.publicitylab.com

233 North Street

Hamilton

New Zealand

Ph: +64-877-9233

Press Release Components

1ˢᵗ paragraph—Summary/overview of press release

2ⁿᵈ paragraph—Brief snapshot bios of producers/musicians

3ʳᵈ paragraph—Features of the release (type of genre, other contributing artists, etc.)

4ᵗʰ paragraph—Contact info

Keep in mind that this is just one example, but it's a good one.

The above is simply a template, but it gives you an idea of the format that magazines are looking for. Magazines are always looking for content, so write a press release and have some friends who are skilled in writing give you some feedback on tightening it up. Once it looks good, send it off. You will get a bunch of rejections, but trust me, someone will say yes. The more magazines you send it out to, the greater the chance you'll have of landing a feature in a magazine. But keep in mind that this is about building relationships, so when you get rejected, be professional about it and thank the publications for their consideration. If you have a project or release you are promoting, set aside time each week to send out your press releases. Even if you hire a PR firm to send out press, I highly recommend that you send them out yourself as well. Think about how many magazines there are in the world. A publicist can't reach all of them, or even most of them. I like to take the approach of doing as much as possible. I have interns who work for me and come over each week. Sometimes they help brainstorm and generate ideas on how to market releases, and other times I have them send out press releases to various dance music magazines around the world. But I also do quite a bit of this myself.

When I have a release I am promoting, below is exactly what I do:

- Hire a record promotion company. My favorite record promoter is Concrete Promo in London. The prices are affordable and the company has a great reputation. The owner of Concrete Promo was the director of one of the most respected record promotion companies in dance music, and a few years ago, decided to start his own company He is among the best of the best and is amazing to work with. When you are ready to have a record promoter, I highly recommend using Concrete Promo.

- During the month of the record release, I send out five press releases to magazines per day. On Wednesday, I send out more than this because this is the day my interns come over, and during a release our focus is on sending out press releases.

- A recent addition to the marketing plan is that we create competitions around the release. For example, it could be a remix competition. Some of you might have heard about the music video competition we recently created for "Freedom." Creating a competition is a great way to engage your friends and fans. If you go this route, there needs to be something that you award them with. If it's a remix competition, the winner is awarded with being on the official release. Any other competition generally involves giving away prizes. For example, we just did a competition in which we gave away free headphones. The company we worked with was willing to donate headphones to give away because we put their logo on the ad that we ran about the competition in *DJ Mag*. If you don't have a budget for something like this, you can give away literally anything you'd like. Just make sure it's something that creates value for the person or people you are giving it away to. You could give away music you've created, a mix, or T-shirts. You could even get in touch with local promoters in your area to see if they would be willing to give you tickets to big concerts they are promoting.

Podcasts

Hosting a podcast is yet another way of marketing yourself in your industry. You can create a podcast that features your music and mixes, or you can create one that features yours along with other artists'. A few years ago we had a podcast called *CyberSutra and Friends*, the name of which we recently changed to that of my record label, Golden Needle Records. I feature my favorite dance mixes from DJs around the world, and promote their current releases. This has been a great networking tool, because it's a win-win situation for the DJs and my record label and a perfect way to cross-promote. I highly recommend doing a podcast, as it's a great way to network and build relationships. In my opinion, the best way to get your podcast going is through the podcast hosting and publishing company Liberated Syndication (www.libsyn.com). It has a reasonably priced monthly rate, and your podcast will be on iTunes. Simply put, you upload your podcast to the site, and they publish it for you so people can listen to your podcast. A nice perk is that your podcast is published to iTunes.

Networking

Now that you are starting to define your structure and vision for what you want to create, it's time to get out there and do it! First, you will need to meet people in your city who are in the same genre that you are in. Become friends with DJs, promoters, club managers, and so on. The best way to connect with these people is if you have a friend who is friends with them. People usually are more open to meeting someone who shares a connection. Friends do business with friends. It's the way the world works. But, of course, it also works to introduce yourself to people—just be friendly and kind.

As far as getting your music to these people, some DJs, promoters, and club managers are open to hearing demos, but most of them are very busy, so it's hard for them to take time out of their busy day to listen to a demo from someone they don't know. Even if they are interested in hearing your demo, their day gets filled with things to do, so oftentimes they will forget to listen. This is where the art of persistence comes in handy. You will need to remind people, but be smart about how often you try to get in touch with them. Don't be a pest. If you e-mail too often, they will become annoyed and will ignore you. E-mailing someone once a week for a few weeks isn't too much. If you still haven't heard from them after a few weeks, then just forget about the connection for a little while. You can e-mail them down the road a bit.

Sometimes a producer will e-mail me their demo, and even if I want to listen to it but I have a lot on my plate, I just won't get around to it. When that producer stays on top of me, I eventually make time because I respect their effort and also know they are going the extra mile. Connecting with these people is the first step in having them hear your demo mix and potentially getting booked for shows. A crucial element to networking is being a good person. Nobody likes an egomaniac, so be cool with people you meet. If you don't get what you want when meeting someone, that's because you are going about it with the wrong idea. Don't look at what you can get out of the situation. Instead, look for the things you can provide them. And when you meet people, all you have to do is smile and be kind to them. Seems simple, but you would be surprised at how many jerks are out there. Don't be one of them, because they are usually the ones who are still trying to be heard or booked.

Post Your Mixes

Here's a great place to post your mixes.

Mixcloud   www.mixcloud.com

A Few Basic Dos and Don'ts

Dos

- Show interest in the person you are meeting. Be engaging by asking them questions about themselves. The more you show interest in others, the more receptive they'll be to what you want. For example, I ask fellow DJs and producers what projects they are working on at the moment. Asking people what they love to do, or what they do in general, is a great conversation starter. Once they tell you, it's simply about asking questions and showing interest. Do you like it when people ask you questions about what you are up to? If you are passionate about what you do, you'll likely love it when someone asks you to talk about what you love. Other people are no different, so ask away. Nothing is more boring than people who talk only about their own interests.

- Smile. Yes, it seems simple, but people who smile attract more people to them. How does it make you feel when someone you are hanging out with is smiling and having a good time? Pretty nice, right? Why not be one of those people who has a positive vibe about them? You'd be surprised at the number of people I meet who have a frown on their face. You are much more likely to be well received if you are smiling when you meet new people. Nobody likes a downer, so don't be one of them!

- What can you give or offer the person you are trying to connect with? Do you have something of value that you can offer? Yes, it sounds counterintuitive to operate this way, as you want them to help you out, but I have found this to be very productive. The best way to network is to give something of value to the people you would like help from. For example, as I mentioned, I have a podcast and I feature certain DJs/producers on my show. I've had a lot of the big-name DJs on the show in the past, so this has been a great way for me to promote and add value to our connection. This doesn't guarantee that they will give you something in return, but it certainly increases your chances. And even if they don't ever return a favor, that person will likely have a generally good feeling about you, and if you are to come up in a conversation they are having with someone, they'll probably have something good to say about you. It's all about creating a positive vibe. Most of the DJs I have had on my show are very responsive to my e-mails and any new tracks I've produced. The reason for this is in large part because I promoted them on the show, so they are more than happy to connect.

Provide value for the people you connect with. Whether it's giving them something special, some free stuff, or doing something for them, it's all about giving rather than taking. Do this, and you will not only feel better about yourself because you will be helping others, but you will also be held in a positive light by the people you do things for. It's a win-win to live this way.

> **Important Note:** If you start feeling resentful while doing this, check your motives. You truly have to come from a place of wanting to add value for others. Don't worry—it'll come back to you, but you've got to check your motives. And if there is someone who you want to connect with and they are not being receptive to you trying to help them out, simply stop and move on. There are plenty of people who will appreciate what you do for them, so connect with the people that appreciate it.

- Be kind to others and check your ego at the door, my friend! Be receptive to those who give you compliments. Did you absolutely kill it during your set? Be cool about it and don't act all high and mighty. In my experiences with meeting some of the best DJs in the world, many of them are humble and kind.

- Someone needs your help with something? Why not help them out? You need help with stuff, too.

- Smile and be engaging.

Don'ts

- Don't be an egotistical jerk. Nobody likes an overblown ego, especially coming from someone who hasn't accomplished much in the DJ world yet.

- Don't expect people to get in touch with you after you first meet them, or sometimes even after the second or third time. Take initiative and save their business cards, so you can get in touch at your earliest convenience. The squeaky wheel gets the grease. One of the most famous DJs in America was someone I wanted to connect with. The whole thing took a few years to materialize, but when it did, it had a profound impact on me as a DJ. I took initiative in that, when he did give me his e-mail address, I contacted him right away. And from there it took time to develop. We connected and it was great, then after a certain point he stopped getting back to a few of my e-mails. Instead of taking it personally, I realized that "Hey, he is one of the busiest DJs in the world—just back off." So, I let it breathe for quite some time and got back in touch with him a year or so later. Now we are in somewhat regular contact, and he's been one of my biggest mentors in the DJ world.

- Don't expect that the people you are reaching out to will always get back to you. People in the music industry are inundated with DJs sending them demos. Make sure to send a reminder e-mail if you haven't heard from someone after about a week. But *do not* bother them every other day with your e-mails. Nobody likes spam.

Chapter Review

Working with a publicist or PR agency is great, but before you get to that point, there is nobody better to advocate for you than whom? You! Develop your writing skills and ability to create press releases. The more buzz you can create on your own, the better. This is how labels, managers, and booking agents will find out about you.

Too often, people approach networking from the standpoint of wondering what they can take from a situation. But if you want to create stronger connections, look to where you can add value. Be open and positive with people. The more approachable you are, the easier it will be for you to navigate through the vast landscape of the music industry.

Exercise

Writing is a great skill to have because DJs/artists write quite a bit. Sound strange? Well, when you want to send your mix demo or music to record labels, you will have to write to them, no? I remember having a conversation with the program director of C89.5 in Seattle, the longest-running dance station in the United States. He told me that he appreciated that he could actually understand my e-mail when I asked to send our music to them. I said something like, "Doesn't every e-mail make sense when you read it?" He said, "Not even close!" The lesson here is that if whoever you want to get in touch with about your music doesn't understand what you are trying to say, then it's likely they will just ignore your e-mail. Besides, as I mentioned before, getting a publicist is expensive, and you are not always going to have enough money to hire one. Writing is a great talent to cultivate, and honing your writing style will help you with your career as an artist. There is simply no way around it, and that's a good thing.

1. Write a press release about yourself using the example illustrated earlier in this chapter. After you finish writing it, have a couple of friends look over it and give you feedback about what you can improve upon.

2. Research podcasts in the genres that you enjoy. Maybe you can start your own?

3. Here's a few podcasts you can check out for ideas on show format.

- *Golden Needle Records*
- *The Opulent Temple Podcasts*
- *Definitive Recordings*
- *Bumpin' House Madness*

4. Find someone this week that you can offer something to. Do not expect or ask for anything in return, simply come up with something that creates value and give it away.

Production

"I think foremost it's not all about pushing the buttons. You need to feel the crowd and adapt yourself to that. You're not only onstage for yourself, but to give the people a great time. The other key, of course, is producing. Get your own tracks out there and get yourself noticed by doing so. Producing is essential as a DJ." —Jesse Voorn

Creating your own music is another key element that will help you expand and promote your name. In today's electronic music world, I would even go so far as to say that it's essential to create your own music. Not only is it one of the best marketing tools out there, but it's fun DJ'ing. The most satisfaction comes when people are dancing to music that you have produced and DJ'd. When you have a song that does well on the charts, it will expand your listener base well outside your home city. Not only is it a good idea to learn how to produce your own music, but it's also essential these days. I strongly encourage you to create your own music.

Obviously, producing music is a skill and craft all by itself. When I started this journey, I decided to go to school to learn sound production. Yes, I wanted to tour the world DJ'ing, but it was creating beats that got me really excited. I wanted to be the guy who was actually creating music that was being played on dance floor. So I started learning how to produce music a couple of years before I got behind the turntables.

If you are interested in producing music, I recommend that you either go to a production school or learn from a friend or someone who is willing to teach you music production skills. The craft of sound production is a lifelong journey, so if it's of interest to you, dig in as deep as you can. To be a great DJ, you don't have to produce your own music, but in my opinion, it will be more fulfilling for you when you are creating tracks and DJ'ing them at your shows. There are many sound production schools around the world, so check around and you'll find the perfect fit.

My personal opinion is that it's not about going to the most expensive school. At the end of the day, after you learn the basics of music production, it's about spending as much time as you can on the craft. Like most things, getting better is about how many minutes and hours one logs into whatever they are doing. It's not about the school you attend, but rather how much energy you dedicate to learning. I went to school to learn production, but I have definitely learned more since I graduated, because I took it upon myself to continue learning to be the best that I could be. With that being said, I am certainly glad that I went to school to get started, because music production truly is like learning a new language.

If you choose to get into music production, below are a couple of things I do, along with the gear I use.

- Before I start a new track, I map out on a notebook how I want the track to sound. I write down some of the things I would like to create with regard to taking notes about what kind of vibe I want to create. This helps me organize my ideas and thoughts on paper first, and gives me a visual map. I also like to log some of the processing, mixing, and EQ settings I am working with in a session. I don't do this with every track, but it is a very effective way to map out your ideas and to save some settings you have going on a particular track.

- Creating music on a computer is fun, but to maximize the creative process and to avoid having the technology make the creative process sterile, it's important that you are able to record your ideas as fast as they come into your thoughts. For example, you don't want to be setting up a synth or bass with all the effects you want when there is a chord progression idea flowing through your thoughts, right? You want to be able to let that inspiration flow and get it down. In dealing with technology there will often be something you'll have to do on the technical side as far as routing something, adding effects, and so on. But the idea here is to at least limit this time as much as possible so you can focus on writing the music. I have a session template that has my main synth settings and instrument saved. Having my most frequently instruments saved in a session template saves me a lot of setup time. It's much better to have a session template with your favorite instruments and processing treatments ready to go. This way, when you have that hook in your mind, you can simply play the parts on your keyboard or punch it in, rather than having to wait to set everything up.

- Once you have your session ready to go, it's time to create music. The first thing I do is get a nice beat and drums going, then I start playing some chords on my keyboard. Once I have a hook that I like, I'll tighten that up and build around that 8-bar "chunk." This is where your map comes in handy. You can build everything around your diagram. This is a great starting point, because instead of having to worry about formatting the entire duration of the track out from the get-go, this allows you to have a nice starting place. Once I have a good 8-bar groove, I spread that out into 16 bars. As I spread and expand the track, then I go back to the original 8-bar section that I loved, and I tweak it.

- Make sure to take your time. I like to spend a lot of hours on each individual track. Some producers pound out a track in a couple of hours, but not me. There is nothing wrong with that approach, but I think it's more effective to create a song that you've given proper attention to. I like to live by the mantra of The Hit Is Written in the Rewrite. Oftentimes I will "finish" a track, only to go back and rewrite it. When I feel I am done with a track, I will let it sit for a few days, a week, or sometimes even several months! Then I go back to it with a fresh perspective and finish it. Sometimes I completely rewrite the track, and it sounds almost like a new track. Other times, I just make big adjustments to it. Not everyone works this way, so play around with different methods until you find what works best for you. I remember reading on Wolfgang Gartner's Facebook page that he spent over three hundred hours creating a track. This might sound discouraging to some people, but I was relieved because it was good to know that other producers like to take their time making music. Wolfgang Gartner happens to be one of the best electro house music producers on the planet, so if you end up making music and it takes you a while to make tracks, don't feel bad at all.

Producing your own music can be very rewarding. One of the best feelings in the world is watching people dance to a track that you made. Of course you don't have to learn how to produce music, but if you want to dive into this industry 100 percent and make it a career, I highly recommend it.

Chapter Review

A big part of the fun of being a DJ is playing songs that you created. Producing is not only rewarding, but is also necessary if you are serious about being a DJ. If you aren't producing yet, find someone who can teach you, or go to school to learn.

Exercise

As I've mentioned, I believe music production is a crucial piece of being in the industry. If you are even considering creating your own music, think of a friend you might have who is already producing music. Now ask if you can sit in and watch one of his or her sessions this week.

Dealing with Rejection

"A great DJ has a passion or obsession for music, and sharing it with others. They're authentic and stand at the edge of something truly amazing. Good DJs create their own sound, something new and different to embrace." —DJ Eva

In any industry rejection is just part of the game, and you are going to hear and see the word "no" quite a bit, especially in the music and entertainment industry. You just have to get used to it. Remember, it's nothing personal and it just means that there is someone else who will say yes to you. Even the biggest and most successful artists still hear the word "no." Tiësto plays the biggest shows in the world, but sometimes a club just can't book him on the night he wants. Granted, he hears far fewer nos than most artists, but it's taken him time to build his reputation. With some practice, you can learn to look at situations objectively. Sometimes you hear "no" because it's a timing issue with whomever you are in communication with. Other times it's a matter of taste. Just because some people say no doesn't mean that there are many people who would say yes. You just have to keep asking until you do find the yeses. They are *always* out there. One way I look at it is that the more nos I hear, the closer I am to hearing a yes. It's about finding the right fit; sometimes you just have to reach out to more people to find the situations that are best for you.

In the Banger Bros and with my solo project, I still hear the word "no," and I am friends with other prominent artists who still go through this challenge as well. So even the best of us deal with this; it's just part of how it works. For example, I remember sending one of our songs to many record labels, all of which rejected it, or just did not respond. One label even went so far as to say that our song would not work on U.S. radio stations. Guess what happened? We ended up signing our song to a New York label, after which it spent ten weeks on the *Billboard* charts. This is perfect example of why you shouldn't take anything personally. It's important to keep going even when it might seem like things aren't working out.

So no matter what, keep plugging away. There is always a yes for you in your future, and you will find the right people to work with. Sometimes it just takes hearing a few too many nos first. No matter what anybody says, you can achieve your dreams. Sometimes it will get difficult and you might feel like quitting, but hang in there.

An important element in staying positive is to surround yourself with a few friends who are supportive of what you are trying to achieve. I've had many meltdowns in the past, when I got discouraged and wondered when things would get better. I tend to have a positive attitude about life, but I am not immune to having a breakdown as well. Sometimes it seems things won't get better, and during the times when I had a hard time seeing that, my circle of trusted friends and family have served as crucial support for me. The more supportive your network is, and the more times you overcome adversity, the more you'll believe that things will get better. For example, now when I am faced with something that I initially see as "discouraging," I trust that it just means something good is coming soon, and that I am supposed to steer in a slightly different direction because there is something better out there for me.

It's key to find a supportive network of friends. You will know who they are fairly quickly, because they are always positive and supportive of what you are trying to accomplish. Anybody who tells you that you can't do something is not someone who you can trust with your dream. Stay away from those people. Or at least don't let them get too close. It doesn't necessarily mean they are all bad. A lot of times they are just stuck in their own lives, and this is the only way of communication they know. At the end of the day, it comes down to your attitude, and a great way to cultivate a positive one with your DJ and music career is to take out time each day to focus on the things that you have accomplished so far. This will help you keep a good perspective about your situation.

Chapter Review

Dealing with rejection is part of the process of being a DJ/artist. There are two things to remember:

- It's not personal.

- Everything in life is simply feedback. Sometimes we get positive feedback, other times we get negative feedback. If you are getting "rejected," look at the experience as an opportunity to grow and adjust, to take a look at what you are doing and improve it. For example, if a lot of people are complaining about your sets and giving you advice on how you can improve them, instead of taking it personally, take it upon yourself to improve your skills as a DJ.

Exercise

Research twenty radio stations and/or podcasts that play the kind of music you want to DJ, and reach out to see if they're interested in featuring your guest mix. After you've reached out to all of them, give yourself a reward for taking action. A massage could be in order, or maybe going to check out a new movie in the theater.

Retaining Your Style

"Great DJs are always reinventing themselves, have very good musical taste and knowledge, patience, and determination to endure the hardships of the profession. [They're] willing to please the audience and make them dance." —Chrizz Luvly

L et's first touch on the topic of music requests. No matter what kind of DJ you decide to become, you will be confronted with this issue more than once. If you decide to be a mobile DJ, who plays at weddings, private parties, and for friends, then taking requests is going to be part of the job description. If, however, you go the route of being a club DJ/ artist, you do not have to take requests if you don't want to. If you go for the latter, the best way to go about dealing with requests is to be kind, and politely tell the person asking for a particular track that you don't have it. It's as easy as that. There's no need to get all pissed off, because that doesn't do anybody good, and you simply don't have to play whatever it is they would like you to. Don't take it personally. I was just playing a show, and before my set I was standing in the booth and somebody asked me if I could ask the DJ to play a certain song. The cool thing was that this person was polite about it. But I didn't even ask the DJ to play it because I knew the answer would be no. This particular DJ was absolutely kicking butt, so it wasn't about them not doing well.

I've mentioned that it's important to be flexible about what you play as a DJ. But I want to make sure I am clear on this. I'm not saying that you should ever play tracks you don't want to. My point is that if you are one of those DJs who like a variety of electronic music, then it's in your best interest to be flexible within that context. If you are planning on being a DJ that plays only techno, then by all means play only techno. Whatever your perspective is on the subject, just be aware of the situations you put yourself in. If you are going to be a techno DJ, don't say yes to a booking where the promoter wants you play some funky house. For example, even though I have a wide range of music I enjoy, if there is a promoter who wants to fly me out for a show but the music the club wants is not something I'm particularly excited about, I'm not going to do that show.

As a DJ/artist, you are going to face choices about what kind of music you want to create and DJ, and what kind of overall style you will put out into the world. A lot of people are concerned about being a sellout and ditching the music they really like for mainstream music. I believe that one should always create and DJ the kind of music that they like the most. If you are following your musical bliss, you will be in alignment with your true desires. There are going to be times when you might have to shift your style to certain crowds. For example, when I play in different countries, I always find out what kind of style of dance music is going over best at the moment. In fact, I had a conversation with a promoter yesterday who told me that right now deep house is big in his country, and he asked if it would be a problem if I played some the next time they brought me out. Was it a problem? Of course not, I love deep house. Now, if he asked me to play country music, I wouldn't do the show. I love a wide range of electronic music, so expanding my scope in that context isn't a problem for me. There are certain styles that I enjoy more than others, but sometimes I am in the minority on a certain genre. For example, I love electro house, but it's not a style that goes over well here in Berlin. If I am playing a show and am playing only music that I love most, then I am missing the point. Again, it's a fine line because you definitely want to stick to what you love—it's just that sometimes you have to be flexible within that context. We are entertainers, and the point is that people who come to the show have a great time. If I am playing music for only my enjoyment, then I should just stay home in the basement.

If you want mainstream success, you are going to have to make whatever it is that you are doing mainstream. In other words, if you create a glitch-hop track that takes the world by storm, perhaps this genre will become the new pop music. Because what's the definition of "pop"? Popular music. The other way to achieve mainstream success is to look into what is currently mainstream and try to do something similar with your own twist. This is the most typical way people achieve this. It's simply about taking the recipe for what is successful and making something of your own that is similar in sound. Sound like copycat work? In a sense it is, and most things in today's world are recycled and reproduced with a different twist. I recommend following your heart and creating what you want. You can't lose if you stay true to what you love most. If that's creating and DJ'ing underground music, stay with that. If you like the idea of creating pop music, go for it.

There is often a lot of talk about the topic of *selling out*. I personally don't believe in this term, because if someone "sells out," then I believe that they are going in a direction that feels right to them. They wouldn't have gone in that direction if they hadn't already liked that style of music. I'm sure some people do it for the money only, and if that's the case, then they probably won't be as happy as someone who is doing it for the love of it. That's true with many things, though. Someone that comes to mind is David Guetta. A lot of people say that he sold out. Many of you may have heard of David Guetta; he is one of the biggest DJs in the world and lately has crossed over into pop music by working with hip-hop artists and pop artists. Back in the day, Guetta was a proper house music DJ with more of an underground vibe. Now that he is mainstream, many people think he is selling out. Music producers and musicians tend to evolve over time, so it's quite common to watch an artist experiment with creating different styles. Most of my DJ/producer friends love all kinds of music, so we love to experiment with making different kinds. My belief is that Guetta truly loves the kind of music he is making and DJ'ing, and if that's the case, he is absolutely not selling out.

A lot of people complain about the mainstream, yet these are the same people who are not buying underground or indie music. They say that the mainstream has no soul, but it's that kind of attitude of judgment that creates a lack of soul. My advice here is to pay no attention to what people think about this topic. It all comes down to what you want to do. Be mindful of every situation you are in, though. If you are into underground music and try to mix in a current pop tune at a show, it's probably not going to work! And if you are like many of my DJ/producer friends, you will not only enjoy music but you will also want to create a wide range of it. Music makers have respect for what it takes to produce music, and a lot of us like to experiment with creating many different kinds of it.

Chapter Review

Figuring out what kind of DJ you want to become is an important part of your journey. It's likely you'll evolve as a DJ/artist, even if you DJ the same kind of music thirty years from now. Explore the different genres and DJ the styles that you enjoy and feel the most connection with.

Exercise

Research your three favorite DJ/artists and pay attention to the kind of music they play, their image, and their brand. What could you incorporate into your style?

Conclusion

N ow it's time for you to discover yourself as a DJ and an artist. The journey of an artist and a DJ is truly a rewarding process, so I'm excited for you as you unleash your passion. Remember, there will be ups and downs and you will be faced with many challenges, but if you stick to your dreams, you'll experience many victories as well. As long as you stay true to what you love the most about DJ'ing, stay dedicated, and practice persistence while keeping an open mind, this will be a journey that enriches your life.

I have covered several tools that will get you started in your pursuit of becoming a DJ who uses live instruments during performance. I have given you the exact formula I use for my success, and I hope it assists you on your journey to achieve your dreams. If you follow these steps, you will be well on your way to becoming the artist that you envision.

Times are changing as fast as ever. People love the idea of mixing technology with the organic. For a long time the music experience was all about live bands. Then the funk and disco eras inspired the DJ world. Today and going forward, people like the combination of both worlds. So being a DJ is not enough anymore. We have the technology at our fingertips to create something new, while reintroducing live improvisation into an electronic music set. The future of dance music is about incorporating your live instrument into your shows and interacting and connecting with the crowd in a powerful way.

This is not a new concept, but the standard is being set for DJs to do more onstage than just putting on a pair of headphones. The possibilities are endless, so it's up to you to find your own unique voice and share it with the world.

And remember to think even bigger than you are already thinking. It's all possible and much more. The tips and knowledge I've passed along to you are from the experience I've gained throughout my career in the music industry. If you practice what you've learned in the book, I am confident that you will achieve success faster than most. It's not like I've been working my entire life to be a DJ/music producer. If you remember, I spent the majority of my youth pursuing a professional baseball career. I mention this because even though being successful takes a lot of hard worked and discipline, if you pour your heart and soul into what you do, you can achieve things at a faster rate.

Being intentional about your vision will speed up the process. I soaked up the knowledge that was passed along to me and learned, and now I'm passing it along to you to do the same. With all that being said, I've been studying DJ'ing and sound production for almost ten years now, and the love of music has been with me since I was a kid. So have patience with yourself and go for your dreams. I look forward to seeing you on the dance floor soon. If you want to see what I am up to, please visit me at www.scottbindermusic.com.

DJ Spotlights

All DJ biographies have been provided by the interviewed DJs or their management.

▶Infected Mushroom

To pioneer your own subgenre of electronic music in the music industry today is no simple task. It is essentially equivalent to Massive Attack effectively originating trip-hop in 1983. Electronic-music, megarevolutionaries Infected Mushroom are renowned for being the sonic innovators of crafting hypnotic arrangements, complex layered melodies, and synthetic rhythms known as "psychedelic trance," leaving behind all their dying "trance" cousins in the mainstream. Twice ranked among the world's "10 Best DJs" by the Bible of the Scene (the UK's *DJ Magazine*), the Israel-bred, Los Angeles–based duo Amit "Duvdev" Duvdevani and Erez Eisen have established their self-invented genre as among the highest in the scene. One could easily scour pages on the Internet in vain trying to find the epic level of music history defining the Infected Mushroom "kingdom." Infected's most notable achievements include their 1999 breakthrough debut album *The Gathering*, which gained immediate attention on club dance floors and in the hands of Goa/psytrance DJs.

Infected's live shows are a spellbinding visual trip that serve as the backdrop for godspeed pumping vocals and banging live instruments. The group's adoring fans continue to descend below Infected's stage en masse at festivals and stadium shows—for example, at Nocturnal Wonderland (in both Texas and Los Angeles), World Electronic Music Festival (WEMF) in Canada, Electric Daisy Carnival (Las Vegas, Nevada), and the Opulent Temple at Burning Man (Black Rock City, Nevada). All walks of life gather in attendance for the same reason: to experience Infected Mushroom, the world's greatest psytrance band of the decade.

SB: What inspired you to become a DJ?
Erez: We have both always been musical, and when playing in our old bands no longer excited us, we teamed up and started making music together. Psytrance was what united us.

SB: What are the three things you think most contributed to your success?
Duvdev: Probably the three things I'd mention are being classically trained as musicians when we were young, having a strong support network of friends and management, and constantly evolving our sound.

SB: What DJ'ing/mixing tip can you provide for readers that will help them become better DJs?
Erez: Find artists you like, and then find the artists they like.

SB: What makes a good DJ?
Duvdev: A good DJ is one who can feel the crowd, and who consistently plays awesome music.

►Judge Jules

Judge Jules is a club DJ, a radio DJ, a music producer, a record company exec, and an entertainment lawyer.

SB: What inspired you to become a DJ?

JJ: The chance to make a full-time living from music isn't an opportunity available to many, as the majority of musicians and DJs do it in a part-time or hobby capacity. The determination to be successful enough that I didn't have to do another (less interesting) job to support my DJ'ing was my main motivation.

SB: What are the three things you think most contributed to your success?

JJ: Amongst others . . . Ibiza, radio, and stage presence—an underrated attribute that not all DJs possess.

SB: What DJ'ing/mixing tip can you provide for readers that will help them become better DJs?

JJ: Keep making your own remixes until at least one-third of your DJ set comprises these. Carving your own musical identity is super important.

SB: What makes a great DJ?

JJ: Talent, marketing prowess, and brains.

►Miss Nine

PHOTO BY SABRINA KORT

Miss Nine was born in Germany as Kristin Schrot, and at the age of sixteen, she started her career—not as a DJ, but as a model. Shortly thereafter, she secured a worldwide contract with Elite Model Management. After moving to Amsterdam she discovered the art of DJ'ing, and her passion for music eventually led her become a DJ as well. In 2003, only a few months after touching the decks for the first time, she became a resident DJ at the legendary Motion parties, where she evolved as an artist and DJ while playing alongside masters such as John Digweed, Dave Seaman, Nick Warren, and James Zabiela.

The year 2005 was when Miss Nine took to the decks as the youngest artist at the tenth edition of Dance Valley (a renowned Dutch dance festival). At the end of 2005, Miss Nine was then asked by Grammy Award–winning DJ duo Deep Dish to join Bullitt Bookings, the reputable agency of A-list DJs. This allowed Miss Nine to enter the forefront of the international DJ scene for the first time.

Fronting her own recording imprint, 925 Music, Miss Nine has created a home for her own releases and a vehicle with which she can sign and bring to prominence artists and music she strongly supports.

Nine Sessions is Miss Nine's monthly radio show, which is broadcasted in more than thirty-five countries, including the stations DI.fm, Proton, Frisky and Dance Paradise. Since January 2011, *Nine Sessions* is also available as a podcast on iTunes.

Today her tour diary continues to be punctuated with performances all around the globe, and she spins at clubs such as Privilege in Ibiza, Avalon in Los Angeles, Warung in Brazil, Ministry of Sound in London, and Pacha worldwide. She has also graced the main stage of Miami's Ultra Music Festival, joining a line-up of, among others, Tiësto and David Guetta. Her recent headline tour of India, alongside Avicii, was another insight into the rising star of Miss Nine as one of dance music's leading female DJs.

SB: What inspired you to become a DJ?

MN: My boyfriend did. He was a DJ and came up with a plan to make me a DJ as well.

SB: What are the three things you think most contributed to your success?

MN: [Being] creative, determined, and consistent.

SB: What DJ'ing/mixing tip can you provide for readers that will help them become better DJs?

MN: Read the crowd.

SB: What makes a good DJ?

MN: Reading the crowd and creating an energetic night

►Kissy Sell Out

One of the UK's finest, Kissy Sell Out continues to be a hugely influential name in electronic scenes all over the world. Whether it's the highly sought-after DJ edits he manages to thrash out four at a time from the Pioneer CDJ-2000s he has helped develop or his charming personality and stage presence, there is a level of mischievous determination about Kissy that seems effortless and genuine. It's this aspect of Kissy's live shows that often divides audiences into those who dance and those who simply stand and stare, with their camera phones held high, as the young DJ speeds through tune after tune before their eyes.

Based in East London, his time between tours is filled with commitments to the independent record label San City High Records. This is a project he founded while still studying at London's University of the Arts, and is the label he now manages entirely from his music studio and Shoreditch office with his like-minded team.

From 2007 to 2012 he hosted a hugely successful BBC Radio 1 show called the *Kissy Klub*. With that radio show, Kissy became an influential force in the developing electro scene not just as a producer but as a tastemaker too. Notable players such as Diplo, Felix da Housecat, Hervé, Uffie, and Erol Alkan made regular appearances alongside exclusive tracks Kissy supported that kick-started careers for a long list of breakthrough producers and DJs across the musical spectrum. His obsessive record-store hunting even earned him the accolades of being not only the first person to interview Skrillex and Ed Sheeran on Radio 1 but also the first ever person to play a Lady Gaga record on national radio!

As crowds continue to flock toward the big man with a big heart and an even bigger sound . . . the party rolls on. Long live the Kissy Klub!

SB: What inspired you to become a DJ?
KSO: I've always felt inspired by music that I don't fully understand. When I first heard a DJ mix it was by DJ Hype, and I remember being fascinated by the level of technical showmanship that was clearly going on in his performance, despite the fact that I had no clue how he was doing it.

PHOTO BY WILL IRELAND 2012

Of course, that is exactly what I fell in love with!

There were moments when the music was pulled backwards over another track, and then released at exactly the right time so that it synced perfectly—and on old vinyl turntables, like my mum had, no less!

There was a spark of curiosity, a hint of mischief, about DJ'ing that I've never lost enthusiasm for. To this day, it is very rare to find anything that can compete with the physicality of dance music in other genres. Oddly, my second favorite type of music is bluegrass country music, simply because it's the only other area of music where technical dexterity and charismatic execution of original music is pushed right to the forefront of the listening experience. It sounds pretentious if you're not already onboard with the idea. It's easy to turn your nose up at someone playing other people's music and labelling it as a performance, but when it's done well, it's impossible to not be swept off your feet by a really talented DJ!

SB: What are the three things you think most contributed to your success?

KSO: I think the only thing I am talented at, musically, is simply being a fan! I used to think my talent was as a composer, since I find writing melodies comes fairly naturally. But as the years have passed, I think the only reason I can do that is because I've learnt to imagine notations in my head from being caught in the rhythmic ideas and inspirations of other people. This is the heritage aspect of electronic music, which makes it community spirited, whilst at the same time, maintains a musically solid foundation. You certainly don't see the same level of risk taking going on in more classical genres.

SB: What DJ'ing/mixing tip can you provide for readers that will help them become better DJs?

KSO: Reedit tracks to fit your style and pace. This is really important. There's nothing more clunky than a track that outstays its welcome. If the best bit of a track is the ending, then only play the ending!

SB: What makes a good DJ?

KSO: This sounds painfully obvious, but honestly, you have to really LOVE the music you play! Scores of unsuccessful DJ hobbyists only play music they think other people want to hear—where's the fun in that? When you really believe in something with a rapturous passion, it is infectious. Surely, that's the secret of a DJ's charisma? DJs can do very little without the power to hold the gaze of an audience.

►DJ Dan

"The thing I love about Dan is that he's always had a funky spirit and he always pushes the elements of music." –Carl Cox

DJ Dan has been synonymous with the American dance music industry for over two decades as a record collector, house innovator, and true legend of the scene. However, his music bandwidth stretches much further; representing the spirit of '70s disco and '80s and '90s house with contemporary flair that makes him like no other artist on the scene. People have been missing the funk, and that's what DJ Dan does best.

Born and raised on the West Coast, Dan was entrenched in music from an early age—1989 to be exact—a time when the rave scene was blossoming. Sharpening his skills spinning vinyl at small clubs in Seattle, Dan's experience in the late '80s behind the decks converted into a profound knowledge of what people want on the dance floor, a trait still ingrained in him today. Many visionary artists have queued up to bottle Dan's unique sound; with a remix discography that reads like a music industry hall of fame, Depeche Mode, New Order, the Pussycat Dolls, and A Tribe Called Quest have all enlisted the boss of breakbeat to tap into his hailed production abilities.

Earning his first Platinum record in 1999, Dan's remix of the Orgy cover "Blue Monday" was revered around the world and reaffirmed his reputation on a global scale, reworking seemingly untouchable records with expert precision. The late 2000s was another period of huge remixes for Dan—most notably, his timeless remixes of "Paparazzi" and "Bad Romance" by Lady Gaga. While dance producers working with pop stars was the thing to do in 2012, Dan preceded the trend by adding his electronic music clout to Janet Jackson's 2010 hit "Make Me." In September of 2010, Dan went on to release one of his finest achievements, his debut artist album *Future Retro*—titled after and the embodiment of Dan's more than twenty years in the industry.

When not in the studio, Dan's playing out all over the world to audiences looking for a proper dance floor education and a great time. Dan's also emerged as one of the most popular DJs at Burning Man, taking the party outside of the club and into the California desert, where much of the American dance scene started.

SB: What inspired you to become a DJ?

DJ Dan: My inspirations started when I was only three years old. I had twin cousins (they were in their twenties at the time) that started buying me records and turntables as Christmas and birthday gifts. This started the trend in my rather large family to buy me new records for all occasions. By the time I hit high school, I had quite a record collection and had become fascinated with DJ'ing. I used to go see DJs like Donald Glaude and Randy Schlager play at the local teen clubs growing up, and by the time I graduated college, I had an amazing record collection and knew I really wanted to become a DJ.

SB: What are the three things you think most contributed to your success?

DJ Dan: Growing up I was drawn to all things funky like Chic, Foxxy, Prince, Kraftwerk, James Brown, etc. By the time house music started coming around in the mid-'80s, I was drawn to the funkier Chicago house sound. I really liked fusing hip house with instrumentals of the records I had been collecting my whole life. After college in 1991, I moved to LA and had developed a sound that was uniquely mine. Fusing all things funky and drawing from my record collection growing up, I had an arsenal of records that I could mix in with newer tracks and this is what really helped me create my own sound. I also used to scratch and mix in hip-hop a cappellas . . . it was a different twist on things at that time, and it really caught the attention of many promoters in Los Angeles.

The second thing was my marketing skills I had learned in college. I started making my own mix tapes and selling them in all the local LA record shops. This not only paid for my records but got my mixes out there to the LA underground.

The third thing that really pushed me heavily into the rave scene in 1993 was my merger with Funky Tekno Tribe in San Francisco. I had moved there to work with a couple of friends that started FTT. This was about pushing a funky new psychedelic sound that was heavily influenced by jazz, hip-hop dubs, disco, acid, funk, and breaks. This sound became so big that I started DJ'ing all across America and eventually joined forces with Jim Hopkins to form the Electroliners. We produced a track called "Loose Caboose" that was played by DJs around the world like Sasha, Carl Cox, and John Digweed, to name a few. This is what really started getting me out to the rest of the world. From there, I started DJ'ing with my good friend Carl Cox who eventually took me on a world tour, and the rest is history.

SB: What DJ'ing/mixing tip can you provide for readers that will help them become better DJs?

DJ Dan: Create your own sound. Don't be afraid to experiment. Music is an art and everyone can tell their own story (even if you are playing other people's music). We play music to inspire people and to make them happy. Pull out the music that makes you happy, and take the crowd on a fun and colorful journey.

SB: What makes a good DJ?

DJ Dan: A good DJ is one that plays from the heart, is not afraid to take risks, and can take the crowd on a great journey during their set. To really care about the overall experience of the crowd that evening and to bring them the best music you have at your access. It can be a fusion of old and new music; it doesn't matter as long as you play a set with passion and love.

▶Todd Terry

Grammy Award–nominated DJ/producer Todd Terry has been engulfed in dance music since he first started listening to European dance music records while growing up in Brooklyn. Already devoted to turntables, he heard something different in those tracks, and he "went for the difference. I never got a break in New York, but England happened right away, so I catered to them." In any event, the Todd Terry sound was born.

By 1988, Todd Terry hit big in England and Europe, and his notoriety was making its way back to the United States. In addition to DJ appearances, Todd was cutting his classic underground tracks "A Day in the Life," "Weekend," and "Can You Party," released under monikers such as the "Todd Terry Project," "House of Gypsies," and "Royal House," all considered essential and groundbreaking.

In the mid '90s, the Ministry of Sound's eponymous UK label released *A Day In The Life*, a collection of Todd Terry tracks that had been causing dance floor panic. That then led the way to a deal with Mercury Records, allowing him to set up a context in which to work with his favorite singers and performers. The first release, "Keep on Jumpin'," on featured a vocal workout from superdivas Martha Wash and Jocelyn Brown, together for the first time

PHOTO BY JOS KOTTMANN

ever. The song became a Top 10 UK crossover pop hit and worldwide smash. Todd followed with the anthem "Somethin Going On," a Top 5 UK crossover pop hit.

All the while, Todd continued to break new ground as a producer/remixer. From SNAP to Annie Lennox to George Michael to Björk, Todd's mixes bridge the ground between club cool and commercial accessibility. In 1995, his remix for Everything But The Girl's "Missing" became a worldwide smash, giving the British duo their first ever hit. He then rode the charts with mixes for Garbage ("Stupid Girl"), the Cardigans ("Love Fool"), Everything But The Girl ("Wrong"), 10,000 Maniacs ("More Than This"), Jamiroquai ("Alright"), the Cardigans ("Been It"), and the Lightning Seeds ("You Showed Me"), among others. He also produced a Robin S track ("Givin' You All That I've Got") for the multi-Platinum *Space Jam* soundtrack.

Todd is one of the world's most celebrated figures in dance music. Currently managing the labels, writing, producing, remixing, and performing more than seventy-five shows a year, Todd is as busy as ever.

With almost two decades of dance floor domination under Todd's belt, the quality of his productions goes from strength to strength. Welcome to the church of house music, presided over by Todd the God. Are you a believer?

SB: What inspired you to become a DJ?
TT: Being at the Brighton Bazaar, fourteen years old, listening to the first DJs I ever heard, Marky B, and DJ Larry. That got me interested.

SB: What are the three things you think most contributed to your success?
TT: Luck and timing are the keys to my success in the music biz, that and getting my break in England before New York.

SB: What DJ'ing/mixing tip can you provide for readers that will help them become better DJs?
TT: Follow the crowd, feel the crowd.

SB: What makes a good DJ?
TT: A good DJ can work the crowd and get a flow going with the previous DJ.

►Olivier Giacomotto

Olivier Giacomotto (born February 2, 1976, in Bordeaux, France) is a French electronic music producer and DJ, and is also known as Superskank, Ohmme, or OG.

He started his career in 1999 and first got into production by working in recording studios where he learned the use of samplers, mixing desks, effects, computers, and music software. From Blues Café studio in Paris to Townhouse Studios in London, Olivier worked with Robert Suhas, Magnus Fiennes, Guy Pratt, Yohad Nevo, Pete Lewis, John Themis, Bond, Lyrics, and various other bands, producers, studio musicians, and sound engineers.

Since 2006, thanks to the success of his productions and remixes such as "Volta," "Gail In The O," "Guacamoli," and "i'll be ok," his name regularly appears in the Top 10 charts of Beatport, the biggest online music store specializing in electronic dance music. The multinational developer and publisher Rockstar Games licensed four of his tracks—"Wasabi on Top," "Good," "Sofa King," and "Too Cool for Skool"—for the top-selling video game Midnight Club Los Angeles. He also produced for pop and reggae artists Terry Lynn and Tom Frager. One of his productions for Terry Lynn titled "Stone" was licensed for the soundtrack of Hollywood box office hit *Date Night* (with Steve Carell, Tina Fey, and Mark Wahlberg) and "Give Me That Love," coproduced with Tom Frager on the major global music company Universal, have been charted during two weeks in the French Top 50 selling thousands of singles and albums.

He currently coruns the independent label Definitive Recordings with John Acquaviva, and works on various kind of music projects around the world.

SB: What inspired you to become a DJ?
OG: In our electronic music world, the studio and the stage are very close from each other, so when I started as a producer, I had to choose between playing my tracks live or as a DJ and it was kind of tricky for me. But one day in 2001, I went out in a club of my hometown and I saw Richie Hawtin playing with the very first edition of Stanton Final Scratch, he was the only one at this time who was able to mix the analog world with the digital world, using vinyls controlled by a computer with samplers and drum machines. A few weeks after, I

bought my own Final Scratch system, and for the first time I was able to produce a track in the afternoon and play it at night—that was a true revolution.

SB: What are the three things you think most contributed to your success?
OG: [First, skills.] Knowledge is a strength. Back in 2000 I learnt how to use all the tools of the production in some of the biggest recording studios in London. [Second,] work. I always worked hard, spending hours in the studio and also at home preparing my set for the stage. [Third, timing.] I think I produced the right tracks at the right time and on the right labels.

SB: What DJ'ing/mixing tip can you provide for readers that will help them become better DJs?
OG: For the ones like me who play with a laptop, try not to look at the screen all the time, except when you look for the next track to play. The crowd needs you to interact, so even if you're shy, look at the crowd, read it, try to understand what it needs in terms of intensity. My secret is to look at the girls and see how they dance. If girls are enjoying your sound, all the boys will follow.

SB: What makes a good DJ?
OG: Being "good" is very subjective. Like good food, a DJ can be compared to a chef in a restaurant; he plays with "ingredients," and the crowd likes it or not. So once you find the right people and the right place where to play your sound, you're halfway to the success.

►Lazy Rich

The year 2012 was an incredible one for Lazy Rich. At the start of the year he was seen as the underdog to watch for, but by the end of it he not only proved that right but also accomplished what is undeniably an incredible leap in success.

A UK native and a resident of Canada, Lazy Rich is heading full steam into 2013, a year that promises to be nothing short of an intense and well-deserved return on an incredible amount of hard work both as a producer and a touring artist.

As a producer, Rich, or "Lazy" as most like to refer to him, has been anything but! In a span of less than five years in the studio, he has scored an incredible number of production successes, both with chart toppers and underground hits with No. 1s on Beatport, Trackitdown, Juno, The Buzz Chart, and over one hundred tracks charting in the Beatport Electro House Top 100.

He has done remix work for such musical icons as Lady Gaga, Fatboy Slim, deadmau5, Chris Lake, Morgan Page, Zedd, Porter Robinson, X-Press-2, and many more while collaborating on tracks with Chris Lake and Porter Robinson. Rich's music has been featured on radio shows such as Pete Tong, Judge Jules, and Kissy Sell Out on BBC Radio 1, while his own radio show, *The Lazy Rich Show*, has become one of the most-listened-to and influential electro house podcasts.

Considered one of the forward-thinking leaders of the electro house genre, Rich is credited for being a pioneer in complextro, a cutting-edge sound on the forefront of the electronic music evolution. His style of gut-wrenchingly intense and audaciously epic house music has put countless big records in his musical arsenal and paved the way for him to create his own signature niche in the market, attracting remix requests from electronic music as well as pop music stars, while television ads and Hollywood films can now be added to that list. In 2013 we can expect to see releases on labels such as Dim Mak / Owsla, Ultra Records and LE7ELS, while his own label, Big Fish, continues its assault as one of the top electro-house labels, priding itself on showcasing new talent, having helped kick-start the careers of Porter Robinson, Zedd, and Lucky Date.

Rich has also been proving his ground as a performing DJ. Having twelve years of experience, teamed with a natural ability to read the crowd and respond with precision, he is quickly gaining a reputation that's setting him apart as a DJ's DJ and a professional rather than the onslaught of the cliché digital DJ generation.

Focused on the US market for the past year, Rich has paid his dues with an incredible coverage of the scene while steadily expanding into the international tour market. Plans for a long-awaited European and Asia tour are in the works for 2013.

With a string of new projects on the way, his first full-scale music video, a long line-up of slated remixes, teamed with an impressive tour schedule in the works, the future looks incredibly bright for this rapidly rising star, who is anything but Lazy.

SB: What inspired you to become a DJ?
LR: I've been listening to dance music from a very early age. I remember my parents buying a technotronic album when I was four, and I used to come home from school every day and listen to dance music on the radio while I played with my Lego. When I got to University a friend and I decided to take the leap and buy some decks just to play around with, and I guess I got kinda obsessed with it and spent every free minute I had mixing. The rest is history!

SB: What are the three things you think most contributed to your success?
LR: I think having a lot of free time and a student load when I started certainly helped me get started, and then having the tools and support network necessary to make the leap into the production side of things. Lastly, my management team for the last four years has been absolutely incredible and have really pushed things to another level.

SB: What DJ'ing/mixing tip can you provide for readers that will help them become better DJs?
LR: I think opening is becoming a bit of a lost art nowadays, and I encourage people to take the time to step back and think about what exactly DJ'ing is about. Too many openers feel the need to impress the headliner by playing the biggest tracks and getting the most interaction, but a headliner really appreciates an opening DJ that shows restraint and leaves room for them to develop their sets properly over the course of the night.

SB: What makes a good DJ?
LR: Without a doubt the ability to read a crowd is key. I see a lot of producers turn up with their preprogrammed sets and the crowds just aren't into it. You have to be able to change things on the fly and respond to the feeling in the room. You also need confidence, stage presence, and to look like you're enjoying yourself!

►Felguk

The Rio-based duo of Felipe "Fel" Lozinsky and Gustavo "Guk" Rozenthal has been blowing away audiences and ears since 2007, lighting up clubs and festivals with their free-for-all mix of electro, house, and heavy low end. The only Brazilians to rank on *DJ Mag*'s Top 100 DJ poll for two consecutive years, 2011 and 2012, the duo has already conquered legions of fans, including star power names like David Guetta, Flo Rida, the Black Eyed Peas, and Madonna, who have all commissioned the duo for potent remix work. The partnership with the Material Girl peaked this year when she personally selected Felguk to accompany her on her full MDNA tour of Brazil, where they performed for sold-out stadium-size audiences.

In 2010 supercharged EDM promoters Insomniac handpicked Felguk's peak-time hit "2nite" as the theme song for the US's biggest festival, Electric Daisy Carnival, breaking records with more than 180,000 partiers. Felguk's appeal doesn't end there. True fans of electronic music, Felipe and Gustavo are concerned with more than just making their mark in the pop world. Recent collaborations with scene highlights like Los Angeles dubstep kingpin 12th Planet, Australia's top house export Dirty South, UK bass fiend Example, and Israel trance act Infected Mushroom prove that Felguk has its ear to the pulse of the global dance scene.

For further convincing, you need only look to the duo's raucous sets at Tomorrowland and Burning Man in 2012, or the full tours of Brazil, Europe, and the USA that will kick off 2013. And Felguk's future plans don't end there. With their first official EP released in March of 2013, Felipe and Gustavo are ready to bring audiences the world over into the sound they have been cultivating for the past five years.

SB: What inspired you to become a DJ?

Felipe: Attending dance music shows when a teen. We saw what a different impact this kind of music had on the crowd. Music that made you move your body almost without even noticing.

SB: What are the three things you think most contributed to your success?

Felipe: Hard work, hard work, and more hard work. It sounds a cliché, but it is true. The road to professionalism is tough, and until you start getting positive feedbacks from whoever, you feel there's nothing that can attach you to this bold option you did in life. At this point, it's not hard to quit when some other opportunities appear, but if you hang tight and keep pushing yourself, your chances increase every day. But don't be fooled, after you find your way to professional EDM producing and expression, you still have to work hard every day. Dance music changes really quickly and you have to always adapt, with the challenge to keep putting out something original and unique.

SB: What DJ'ing/mixing tip can you provide for readers that will help them become better DJs?

Gustavo: The best advice to make you stand out is to be a producer as well. Not only you will start to understand the music to new depths, but that will give out a lot of credibility among the public. They want to see who made that beat that they love so much.

SB: What makes a good DJ?

Gustavo: Besides all that was said before, I would add . . . having fun! The DJ life seems very magical and to some point it really is, but after some years of heavy touring you can really start feeling that DJ'ing is a real job, LOL. Always look for tracks and vibes that you genuinely love so that you can really feel it when you play out to the crowd. They will feel your joy, and the whole energy is gonna flow easily.

►Umek

It would take a long essay to fully explain UMEK's meaning to electronic music. The Slovenian-born producer and DJ has been setting trends and rocking dance floors for two decades now, and still shows no signs of slowing down. He's tireless in his techno and tech house production, and with more than one hundred gigs per year is probably one of the busiest techno DJs out there.

He's not only been rocking our ears with his own productions for labels like Toolroom, Spinnin, Great Stuff, Intec, and many more, but has also been heavily involved in choosing who to sign to his arty imprint 1605, which mostly supports young and talented artists who haven't yet made it on the global party scene.

Having conquered most of the world's biggest stages and festivals, UMEK started his own weekly radio show *Behind the Iron Curtain*, which immediately landed on dozens of the world's hippest EDM radio stations.

Although he probably holds a national record for the number of flights per year, UMEK still finds time for charity. Every August he hosts a charity event called Party with a Cause, where local sponsors help raise money for a certain cause, mostly to help underprivileged youth.

SB: What inspired you to become a DJ?

U: Two things, actually. The first one was the music: I really liked all these new electronic sounds, and at the same time I was intrigued how this music's been created, which for me was almost impossible to get to know at the time (late '80s when I got in touch with acid house), as there was a big lack of this kind of knowledge and the information about this new scene in Slovenia. I was really hooked on this music, and I wanted to learn the ways to produce and mix it.

The second incentive was the role of DJ. At some school dance I watched DJ Alf (a colleague of mine who later taught me basics of mixing and gave me the first chance to perform in his club), who at the time mixed music from tape cassettes and he played what he wanted and people responded to his program having fun on the dance floor. He was a king of that party, and I admired him as he offered people his own music selection and at the same time he had total control over the dance floor. So, the inspirations were music and the role of the DJ and his power to control the room.

PHOTO BY CIRIL JAZBEC

SB: What are the three things you think most contributed to your success?

U: The most important was my stamina, endurance, determination. I've never thought of myself to be a very talented artist, so I have to compensate that with a strong working ethic, discipline, and motivation. I used to spend up to fifteen hours daily in the studio; there was a time I went home just to take a shower, eat, and sleep. I still remember the times when I was sweating in the studio day after day on a diet of Coca-Cola and potato chips. I've seen people around me getting their music released much easier, but I needed that time to work hard, to try new equipment, to test new approaches and inventing things on my own to get the results I wanted.

The other thing was the courage to follow my passion. I was a really perspective basketball player and I was still in the high school when I decided to drop both and focus on one thing only: to become one of the top international DJs and producers. At that point I put everything I had into it, but my mother was disappointed because my dreams seemed impossible. Though later she noticed how dedicated I was to this goal and she supported me all the way. Although I've made it to the top, I would not recommend young people to follow my lead, as the chance of success is one in thousands and I believe in general it's good to have some kind of education. I was lucky to know quite early in my life what I wanted. I was very dedicated and also lucky to succeed. But the end to this story could easily be very sad.

SB: What DJ'ing/mixing tip can you provide for readers that will help them become better DJs?

U: There are a couple of things that make a good DJ: a very good music selection and programming of the night, top-notch technical skills, and a good contact with the crowd on the dance floor. These three things are essential for success, and you will succeed at one point of your career if you have these knowledge and skills. But you have to be dedicated and keep pushing, especially when it's hard, as success rarely comes overnight. Sure, there are exceptions to this rule, there are guys who are extremely talented or have a big luck to break through as a supernova, but most of the DJs that are considered today's leaders of the scene worked really hard to get where they are today.

SB: What makes a good DJ?

U: Stamina, endurance, and determination.

▶Format:B

Format:B are Franziskus and Jakob. Jakob is a Berliner, from Kreuzberg to be exact. As all good parents do, his wanted him to play an instrument. After years of successfully dodging music lessons and his parents' wishes, Jakob finally at the subtle age of fifteen decided that he desperately needed a bass guitar, which then through diligent practice he used to maneuver himself from hardcore bands to funk and jazz bands.

PHOTO BY ANDREJ DALLMANN

But suddenly, there was a small problem: he liked techno parties much better than rock concerts. So, as one does, he began buying the odd techno maxi here and there until one day little Jakob thought to himself, "Why heck, I can do that, too!" So off he went and bought himself an overpriced Atari St40 and a cheap synthesizer, only to realize that—oops!—those guys from Detroit really do know what they're doing and that it wasn't that easy after all. Well, that is basically where Jacob's ambitiously planned-out life suddenly took a screeching-of-the-wheels turn in another direction.

Franziskus is from Erfurt, a small and rural part of Germany's quite rough and wild East, which didn't stop him from starting piano lessons at the innocent age of six. His musical interests took him from the usual suspects like Michael Jackson and the Pet Shop Boys through to hardcore (obviously not on the piano). But then one day (or night, to be exact), similar to Jakob, all was to suddenly change. A fortuitous night out at the legendary E-Werk in 1993 made this young man's heartbeat skip from Chopin over to a 4/4 beat, where it was to remain, probably forever. Three years later Franziskus took up residency at the infamous Sub Ground Lighthouse After Hour, resulting in numerous further bookings. The paths of these two young men crossed whilst they were both studying to be sound engineers. Seeing as all the other students in their year were longhaired metal heads, it was only a matter of time until their paths crossed. So, after spending a few long Berlin party nights together, they decided to see if they could start a project together. And so the story ends—or better yet, begins—with Format:B.

After they were banging numerous hit singles like "Vivian Wheeler," "Edding 850," and many others, they decided to found their own label, Formatik Records, in August 2009. In addition to that, they built up a new studio in Berlin Prenzlauer Berg to work on their second album, called *Restless*. Meanwhile they checked out a lot of brilliant techno artists like Sébastien Léger, Hugo, and Super Flu to work with. Super Flu were remixing the track "Gospel"—an outstanding club hit, which finally brought Formatik Records to the ears of the world. As a consequence of their great success, Jakob and Franziskus were "forced" to play live on the whole planet. So they toured Australia, Asia, the USA, and discovered their biggest fan base in South America. In Berlin they found the Watergate Club as the best place to celebrate their own label events.

SB: What inspired you to become a DJ?

Franz: In the early '90's some of my friends have already been DJs. So I always found it desirable to play your music in front of a big audience . . . and hopefully getting good feedback by the people. Also, I liked the idea of traveling around a lot and spreading your music in the whole wide world.

Jakob: Actually, I came to DJ'ing more or less by accident. After just listening and dancing to techno music for some time, the wish came up to make my own tracks. Producing with Franz led to our first release and first live act . . . after four to five years of playing strictly live, I felt that the limited selection of tracks started to bother me more and more . . . so this was the main aspect which inspired me to become a DJ. And since then I really don't want to miss the freedom and intuitiveness of it anymore.

SB: What are the three things you think most contributed to your success?

Jakob: I think the fact that we are a duo helped us in many ways. In our case we both feel that our abilities complement each other well. When working on a track, this means that together we can get this extra 10 to 15 percent to make it perfect. Four ears just hear more than two! This directly leads me to the next thing: our own style.

In studio we always just did whatever we both liked . . . and the result was what you might call a trademark sound . . . indispensable to get recognition as a newcomer act. As a third thing I maybe name something sounding very generic, but I really believe that this is also an important part of our story. Stay down to earth, don't take yourself to serious, be appreciating, and at least always try improve yourself.. . .

SB: What DJ'ing/mixing tip can you provide for readers that will help them become better DJs?

Jakob: I would name that it doesn't matter if you play vinyl, CD or digital. The medium is not affecting your ability as a DJ. A very common belief is that people think using Traktor would enable them to play great sets. It just helps the beatmatching; your taste of music and inspiration in the moment stays the same! Already great or still crappy.

SB: What makes a good DJ?

Franz: In my opinion a good DJ takes the risk of trying something unconventional sometimes. He has a great sense for the atmosphere and audience of the night and reacts to it in his selection.

Jakob: For me it's a kind of similar thing as with producing.
A good DJ has his very own idea or vision. If you think of your five personal favorite DJs, I think you can immediately draw a specific sound/vibe to them . . . but this "personality" is something you either have or not. You can't really learn it like mixing techniques.

►Hirshee

Hirshee was born and raised in one of Canada's most diverse cities—Vancouver, BC. Immersed in such a society where the people and cultures he experienced were in a constant state of flux, Hirshee learned early and quickly the fruits of being open-minded. Growing up, he was especially unprejudiced with regard to his musical tastes, listening to a boundless variety of genres and styles.

Today, the influence is not subtle, as this very diversity is what differentiates Hirshee from the rest of the pack. The hard-hitting DJ has become renowned for his array of tracks and unpredictable beats that cannot be defined to only one genre in the electro realm. Since 2006, Hirshee has been pumping out brilliant hits that feature a dynamic blend of melodic prowess, memorable vocal hits, and complex, thrashing bass. While some artists need to be discovered, Hirshee was simply impossible to ignore. This has led to his tracks getting airplay on the legendary BBC Radio 1 and support from artists like Tiësto, Fatboy Slim, Steve Aoki, Chris Lake, DJ Dan, Calvertron, Lazy Rich, Hatiras, Dirtyloud, Will Bailey, and many more.

As things began to take off, Hirshee did not hesitate to take advantage. Teaming up with the talented Lazy Rich and starting Big Fish Recordings, the duo quickly raised the name to prominence, making it one of the leading electro labels today.

Hirshee broke out at the turn of the decade with chart-topping bangers like "The Rinse Out," "Always Tomorrow," "Big Life," and "California." However, the track that best defines him is the wildly popular "So Good," a collaboration with the soulful Tonye Aganaba. Thanks to Aganaba's dreamy yet haunting vocals and Hirshee's dazzling and powerful drop, the song topped out at No. 1 on Beatport's Dubstep Chart for three weeks.

Hirshee's music takes you for a ride, as you travel through detailed ebbs and flows of synth leads and potent bass. The destination is uncertain since, as his growing international recognition and worldwide booking requests demonstrate, the trip has only just begun. This is your chance to get on board; Hirshee has arrived.

SB: What inspired you to become a DJ?

H: Music has always been a big part of my life. I started out playing drums and some piano, but once I heard electronic music for the first time I knew I had to be a part of it somehow.

SB: What are the three things you think most contributed to your success?

H: Hard work, a strong passion for music, and patience.

SB: What DJ'ing/mixing tip can you provide for readers that will help them become better DJs?

H: Don't preplan/prerecord your mixes. Different crowds like different things, so having room for flexibility in your set is key.

SB: What makes a good DJ?

H: Creativity, ability to read crowds, and strong track selection.

▶Manuel De La Mare

Tuscan-born producer/DJ Manuel De La Mare has spent the past twenty-four months delivering money-shot releases and remixes, whilst marrying a lifetime of passion and dedication to his love of DJ'ing. This ability within his musical sphere has pricked the interest of global artists like Mark Knight, John Acquaviva, and Feddle Le Grand, who have all requested his studio talents, whilst leading Beatport to bestow him the award of Best Remixer 2011—a suitable follow-up on his nomination for Best Deep House and Techno Artist back in 2010.

Emerging as one of Italy's forward-thinking music creatives, Manuel formulated his own sound by fusing together elements of varying genres that have long been the aural identity of his native country. Combining Italo dance, jackin' filtered and deep house, rolling techno beats and crossing minimal melodies, Manuel has been able to construct a unique musical presence that is both eclectic and flexible yet robust and cutting edge—a characteristic very much found with his studio releases.

Manuel, now with doctorates in music, cinema, and theater under his belt, has progressed from being an unknown artist to becoming one who circumnavigates the globe performing and releasing his music to thousands of fans in an incredibly short time. This makes it understandable why he's able to count among his biggest supporters international doyens such as Bob Sinclar, Richie Hawtin, Paul Van Dyk, Carl Cox, Axwell, and David Guetta.

Throughout Europe, Asia, the Middle East, Africa, and North and South America, his sound stretches somewhere between house and techno, whilst respectfully treading the line between commercial and credible underground. The successful year was settled also by the two extremely played releases, which have been on demand for months. Yeah, one of them is definitely "Opa Locka"—his collaboration with his partner and 303lovers/Hotfingers coowner Luigi Rocca—and his house remix for "I Love The Music"—made together with the other colleague, Alex Kenji—that was one of the best house tracks of March and April 2012. Partners in music production, the Italian trio now gathers behind the DJ booth creating their future project, called Forza, and it's meant to shake the dance floor in the near hereafter. All Manuel's roaring progress has naturally evoked his nomination for the Best Remixer of the Year, which followed up his winning position of the same contest for the previous 2011 year.

SB: What inspired you to become a DJ?

M DLM: My life is a circle made of nights listening to music, parties, clubs, smiling people, people dancing, grooves, making grooves, traveling, traveling in exotic places, coming back home, and making more music. My love for all this made me a DJ.

SB: What are the three things you think most contributed to your success?

M DLM: A big unconditioned love for music that made me go over all difficulties I found on the way; thousands of hours spent studying, making and listening to music; and, the most important, the support from the people that enjoy my music in all the world.

SB: What DJ'ing/mixing tip can you provide for readers that will help them become better DJs?

M DLM: I would advise to spend less time looking at the mixer and more time looking at the crowd.

SB: What makes a good DJ?

M DLM: Make people dance, make people happy, and all this during a whole night, having a journey through different emotions.

▶Joyce Muniz

Joyce Muniz is a Vienna-based Brazilian DJ, vocalist, and producer, who is currently one of the leaders of a new undefined musical style that fuses European club sounds with tropical rhythmic influences from Brazil, South America, Africa and the Caribbean, while built on a solid foundation of percussion and heavy bass.

Born in 1983 in São Paulo, Joyce Muniz arrived in Vienna during the mid-'90s and was soon introduced to the vibrant Viennese electronic music scene. Shortly after her first DJ gig at the tender age of sixteen, she began collaborating as a vocalist with Markus Dohelsky aka Shanti Roots (Vienna Scientists) and I-Wolf (Sofa Surfers/Klein Records). In 2006, Muniz teamed up with Stereotyp and created the first Funk Mundial 12-inch "Uepa/Jece Valadao" (Man Recordings) and Ku bo Ep 1 and 2. In 2007, she and Shanti Roots started producing under the name of Monte Laa Prod and released their first 12-inch.

In 2008 she contributed her vocals to the Cusmos (Herwig Kusatz ad Karl Möestls) track, "Garoto," which was released on the Kruder & Dorfmeister label G-stone. Joyce Muniz also did some collaboration with Flore, Buscemi, and Skero. Her first solo release, "Party Over Here," debuted in November 2010 on Shir Khan's well-known label, Exploited, and received massive DJ support throughout Europe. *DJ Mag* has hailed it "the electro single of the month." Joyce Muniz is featured as a singer on the current Munk album *The Beat and the Bird* out on Gomma, she remixed the classic house anthem "Lovely Daee" by Blaze out on Defected, and just scored No. 4 in the Deep House Beatport Charts with her single "Malicia."

In addition to her DJ'ing and production work, Joyce earned an Amadeus (Austrian equivalent to a Grammy) for her vocal work with Austrian rapper Skero on the hit single "Kabininparty." which won the Best Song of the Year award, as well as winning two other nominations.

SB: What inspired you to become a DJ?
JM: When I started to listen to electronic music, I was fourteen years old and it was the mid-

'90s in Austria. At that time Austria was the capital of downtempo, and Vienna was a kind of a music hotspot so we had a great scene of not only downtempo, but house, techno, and jungle was quite big, too.

I was inspired by all these great DJs and producers around me, and after seeing a lot of shows in Vienna, I started to buy all my music on vinyl. Step by step I bought my first 1210, started playing at private parties, and a few years later I became a resident DJ of Dub Club Mondays at Flex. Dub Club was at the time one of the most interesting and eclectic weekly club nights, so I had chance to meet a lot of great artists, and learn the skills.

SB: What are the three things you think most contributed to your success?
JM: Well, I think I am a good listener; I really like to play for the crowd is what I mean. I don't mind playing a good bootleg sometimes in my set just to see people singing the line of an old-school tune.

Also, I really like to party with the crowd, and this was actually one of the reasons I became a DJ. I hate those robot DJs; they don't move—they don't even watch the crowd!

SB: What DJ'ing/mixing tip can you provide for readers that will help them become better DJs?
JM: When I started to DJ, nobody was playing with computers or CDJs. At the time, we needed to practice a lot to find the tempos and to know each record. So definitely practice as much as you can.

And if you are a new DJ on Ableton or some other DJ software, then please guys, at least take the time to make proper cue points so the mixes blend nicely.

SB: What makes a good DJ?
JM: There are a lot of good DJs, very few great ones. I think having good taste is the most important thing. But being able to read a crowd and adapt your style to make them dance more, without sacrificing this good taste, is what makes a DJ great.

▶Federico Scavo

DJ/producer Federico Scavo's track "Strump" reached Gold record status in Italy in 2011, and Federico has followed this success with his recent new singles "IRobot" on Toolroom, and "Funky Nassau" on DVision. Scavo (www.federicoscavo.com), active all over the world, is unstoppable. Downloads of "Strump" on Beatport, the music download site used by DJs, are about 4,500, while on iTunes Italy are about 14,000. On the main music download site, the track reached No. 2. It's a great result, achieved in a country where people usually don't buy music and where dance music has still not reached the size of pop, as instead happened in other countries.

"During the day, I'm in my recording studio, where I look for new sound and new ideas. Here, I make remixes for 'cult' and underground labels as Ultra Records, Tiger Records, Toolroom Records, Hotfingers Records, or Great Stuff Recordings. I'm really happy with the results: five remixes in Top 100 on Beatport, and if that is not enough, my label, Area94 Records, is in progress."

As a DJ, Federico Scavo is living in a great period. "During spring 2013, I'll be at Tenax in Florence and in Puglia, that's the Ibiza of Italy. I'll be in Miami, Honk Kong, and in Bora Bora Ibiza, too."

Only a few weeks ago, he was in the lineup of the Ultra Music Festival in Miami and in the DJ booth of Ministry of Sound London, a festival and a club worldwide famous. In 2013, he performed at Ruby Skye in San Francisco, at Armani Privee in Dubai, and at Nikki Beach Miami, confirming the international dimension of his career.

SB: What inspired you to become a DJ?
FS: My father is a musician and a singer, so I grew up with music ever since. Then music became a passion, and I started to play for my friends at home parties. It was then I realized that DJ'ing would be my first goal and my profession for life.
SB: What are the three things you think most contributed to your success?
FS: Success is a mix of things. For me I think it depends on the way you work, professionalism, humility, and continuous effort.

SB: What DJ'ing/mixing tip can you provide for readers that will help them become better DJs?
FS: The most important thing is to search for something that identifies yourself and your sound that makes you different from other DJs.

SB: What makes a good DJ?
FS: First of all making as many good productions as possible to provide worldwide visibility, and once in the DJ booth try to enchant the dance floor with your sound.

►Beltek

It seems there's nothing one of the EDM scene's hottest young stallions couldn't turn into gold right now. In just a couple of years since he won Pete Tong's competition with "Copacabana," Beltek's name regularly pops out on top of EDM music charts and labels such as Dim Mak, Ministry of Sound, Toolroom, Armada, Netwerk, and so on. His versatile production skills and fingerprint mass appealing sound already assured him remixing duties for major artists such as Faithless, Booka Shade, Gareth Emery, and many others.

Tiësto picked up "Kenta" for *In Search Of Sunrise 7: Asia* compilation and supported Beltek in the "15 Minutes of Fame" slot of his *Tiësto's Club Life* radio show. Standout productions such as "Par," "Kenta," "Eclipse," "Go," and "Party Voice!" are heavily played, rotated, charted, and compiled by leading artists, radios, and labels and his never-ending touring schedule is taking him all over the world, from Mexico and Spain to the Ultra Music Festival Miami, Amsterdam Dance Event, or Ukraine's infamous Kazantip. On top of that, Beltek's "Party Voice" served as the official track for the Ultra Music Festival Miami remix competition in early 2012. Yes, you got it! Beltek is on fire right now and he's doing big steps on the global EDM scene. So watch out, as he'll definitely mark 2013!

SB: What inspired you to become a DJ?
B: It was actually years ago, when I first saw and heard Jeff Mills playing live on three decks and also including his Roland TR-909 [drum machine] skills in his set.

SB: What are the three things you think most contributed to your success?

B: The first one would definitely be passion for producing and playing music in general—I simply cannot live without it. The second thing would be dedication and persistence, which told me never to give up on my dreams, no matter what. And the third thing is that this job is a lot of fun to me, because there are times when this dream job can also get extremely hard and then when you arrive at the venue, start playing records, and make people have the time of their life, it is something you really need to appreciate. Moments like these are a drug to me and they make me smile.

SB: What DJ'ing/mixing tip can you provide for readers that will help them become better DJs?

B: My advice would be to always start your sets with no kick, beats, so it's just some pad, sphere of sounds going on with uplifting effects which start to rise and rise for about a minute and then the kick and bass punch in. For me that's the basic rule of my live DJ set. Of course if you don't have an intro like that in your record collection, produce the intro by yourself, so you can be unique.

SB: What makes a good DJ?

B: I think the most important thing in DJ'ing and what makes us DJs different from each other is the ability to read the crowd, which also means you will need to have a big collection of records with you (which in these days' technology isn't really a problem) so you can choose your next record that will continue your musical journey that night, but will also entertain the crowd. In the end you are there to entertain the crowd, not to entertain just yourself.

▶Chus (Stereo Productions)

When hard work and talent go hand in hand, the outcome can only be quality. Chus is a DJ, producer, remixer, founder of Stereo Productions, and creator of the pioneering Iberican Sound, a delicious mix of hypnotic organic house elements, warm and intense with a strong tribal essence that fuses naturally with modern tech house.

An extensive self-taught career based on a long-lasting belief in quality music has led to a consolidated position as one of the world's most acclaimed artists. His many awards from the Spanish media include DJ of the Year, Best House DJ, Best House Producer, Best House Label, and Best Remix of the Year, among others, as well as being one of the first Spanish DJs to make the *DJ Mag* Top 100 list. This is reflected in his surprising DJ sets, which range from large festivals to intimate small clubs either as marathon sessions or the typical club slot. He takes his audience on an extraordinary musical journey, from deep to techno and back again, drums always present.

Also, his extraordinary studio work has culminated in a recording legacy of over twenty years in the form of original productions or remixes, whether solo, with David Penn, or Pablo Ceballos, or one of his many other partners in crime. As well as all this, he also fronts his own radio show, the *Stereo! Radioshow*, which can be heard live on the best radio station sites via the Internet or in a weekly podcast version.

SB: What inspired you to become a DJ?
Chus: My love for music! Music has been part of my life since I was very young, because from an early age I would listen to my father's record collection. He was into the classic disco sound, so I've grown up listening to bands like Earth, Wind & Fire, Chicago, Chaka Khan, Donna Summer, Barry White, or The Jacksons, to name but a few. I have fond memories of this music; when I had fourteen years old, I would take my father's tape recordings on cassette and edit them by cut and pasting, then I started to scratch his vinyl records! So you could say they were my first DJ experience and the beginning of all of this.

PHOTO BY ROBERTO CASTAÑO

SB: What are the three things you think most contributed to your success?

Chus: First of all, my love and full-time dedication to music; my passion for music allows me to enjoy every single second of my career, and I love to transmit this feeling to my audience. Then the creation of my benchmark, the Iberican Sound, that have pinned Spain and the Spanish artists on the global EDM map. And for sure the conquest of the American market, one of the biggest and most important ones for me.

SB: What DJ'ing/mixing tip can you provide for readers that will help them become better DJs?

Chus: I prefer to provide a personal tip, first of all, to be patient—you have to devote hours working on it, nothing happens by accident, it's all about the time and effort. And it is also very important to connect with your audience, to be interactive, to look at them and smile!

SB: What makes a good DJ?

Chus: So many small details can lead you to become a good DJ. You have to be able to connect with your audience. You have to "read" what they expect from you and give it to them, you have to create your own way to be followed—not to follow others. As Danny Tenaglia said, Be yourself, and no one else.

►Charles Feelgood

Point blank, Charles Feelgood loves music, and even more, he loves sharing it with his fans. The man prides himself on his ability to connect with his audience—through a wicked combination of his exuberant personality and his exquisite ability to know what fills and keeps a dance floor pumpin'.

His rise to dance music infamy dates back to his humble beginnings as the leading force behind the Baltimore/Washington DC electronic music scene. Alongside his partner and fellow DJ, Scott Henry, Feelgood launched Fever, which for nearly a decade became one of the most sought-after events for touring DJs from around the world.

It was the days after starting Fever that Feelgood enhanced his reputation among those the international dance community. He parlayed his danceable brand of house music up and down the East Coast and became renown for his creative ability to incorporate his love of '80s music with a variety of different house styles into his sets. In the years that have followed, he has taken his talents to all ends of the earth—from North and South America to Russia and Asia, and everywhere in between. He has appeared at such seminal events as Coachella and Lollapalooza, and has become a welcome fixture with Insomniac, Giant, and Karma Foundation. He also plays quite regularly in Los Angeles (Vanguard, Playhouse) and San Francisco (Ruby Skye), and has been a part of the annual Mardi Gras festivities in New Orleans for over a decade.

Around the turn of the century, Feelgood moved from the familiarity of his East Coast domain to sunny SoCal. Since the cross-county relocation, he has become ensconced in the West Coast scene and ramped up his production work. His initial popularity was assisted thanks in part to his legendary mixed series "Time to Get Ill," and has continued to flourish though the release of remixes and singles such as "Hands," "Aerobic Martini," "Strobe Light," and "Burnin'." He is a mainstay in the Top 100 on BeatPort and Top 10 on a number of other worldwide digital sites.

PHOTO BY NATHAN PHILLIPS

Accolades such as repeatedly being named to *DJ Magazine*'s Top 100 DJs aside, Feelgood remains committed to lighting up dance floors around the world—summing up his musical mission in one sentence: "I just want to do what [my] name implies, to make people have a good time and go home with a great feeling."

SB: What inspired you to become a DJ?
CF: My father inspired me to become a DJ. He used to be the family DJ of sorts—always playing Motown and disco records all hours of the night.

SB: What are the three things you think most contributed to your success?
CF: I listen to music all day, every day, and all kinds of music. Growing up in the '70s was such a "feel-good" time. I remember watching my relatives dance and sing at family gatherings—people were a lot more carefree back then. I really wanted a job where I could travel and be my own boss—voila!

SB: What DJ'ing/mixing tip can you provide for readers that will help them to become better DJs?
CF: Practice with real turntables! Computers and software can be fun, but learn the basics and the art form first—then you really can appreciate it.

SB: What makes a good DJ?
CF: Making the crowd happy and you happy at the same time. Too many guys try to only please themselves (there's a joke there) or only the crowd. Do both—you can't go wrong!

►Moonbeam

Graceful and elegant. Exotic and muscular. These adjectives can be just as easily utilized to describe Moonbeam's unique style of electronic dance music (EDM) as they can be used to describe the artists: brothers Pavel and Vitaly Khvaleev. Hailing from Russia and forging the amazingly successful Moonbeam alias in 2003, the act has had an impressive run of more than 177 releases, including original productions, remixes, and three full-length studio albums.

Additionally, the video and graphics arm of Moonbeam's creative organization has produced as many as eighteen commercial-grade music videos. *The Secret* is Moonbeam's third

PHOTO BY ANNA KHVALEEVA

and latest full-length studio album, released in November of 2011. It's no wonder that, for the third year in-a-row, Moonbeam has placed on the venerable *DJ Magazine* Top 100 DJs poll in 2011—quite an accomplishment considering the tens-of-thousands of DJs around the world vying for a slot.

With a musical style described as existing somewhere in the netherworld between atmospheric trance and high-octane techno, Moonbeam's live shows are a multisensory treat. Playing together in the world's top clubs and festivals since the duo's inception in 2003, Moonbeam have worked hard to establish and grow a dedicated fan base amassed from all corners of Europe (in particular, France, Italy, and the Netherlands) and Asia (Japan and India, in particular). With their first hardcore foray into the North American dance music scene in 2011, the duo is also preparing to take this continent by storm.

As their astounding discography attests, the members of Moonbeam are not only some of the most prolific EDM artists to emerge from Russia this decade, but they are also among the most sanguine.

SB: What inspired you to become a DJ?
Vitaly: The best feeling that you can feel as a DJ—watching crowd reaction. And when people are getting crazy while you're playing behind the decks—that's, maybe, the best part of a DJ's career. So, probably this was the reason.

SB: What are the three things you think most contributed to your success?

Pavel: Perseverance, hard work, and the most important: love what you do.

SB: What DJ'ing/mixing tip can you provide for readers that will help them become better DJs?

Pavel: Listen to more good music, love music and people.

SB: What makes a good DJ?

Vitaly: Continual improvement of your DJ skills.

►Quentin Mosimann

Quentin Mosimann proved that he has not even scratched his fifteen minutes of celebrity fame. Difficult to pinpoint and unexpected, here is an artist who can be discreet while always surprising us with new discoveries. Today, after a double Gold record in 2009, Today, after a double Gold record in 2009, he's been elected No. 74 of DJ Mag's worldwide top 100 poll for 2012.

Between his electro house and progressive style, this DJ, remixer, and producer has proven his talent as a musician, a DJ, and especially a vocalist, always entertaining the public. He won the French Pop Idol (*Star Academy France*) in 2008, but this is not the reason why all the clubbers wait for him and come from everywhere to enjoy his exhibition at each club and festival. You find his originality through a direct interactivity with his audience, struck by an atypical voice and the flights of his synthesizer.

This DJ who sings, motivated by the desire to surprise, has created his own eclectic innovative style, offering to the most skeptic the capacity to change without notice, and offering the nonskeptic the satisfaction of an exceptional show.

SB: What inspired you to become a DJ?
QM: Sharing in a different way. DJ'ing has no frontiers, no boundaries. I was fifteen years old and I had a revelation when I saw Joachim Garraud for the first time. He was bringing something different, special, a real connivance with the audience.

SB: What are the three things you think most contributed to your success?
QM: Most of all, I'm lucky to have a great community supporting me and believing in me since the beginning. Then, I tried to offer a real show at every performance, with energy, singing, and keyboard: being a DJ singer and a performer is the basis of my job. And finally, I keep the flame and passion every day no matter what, maybe it helps . . .

SB: What DJ'ing/mixing tip can you provide for readers that will help them become better DJs?

QM: You have to find the balance between finding your own style and satisfying the crowd. I think this is what DJs forget sometimes: they're here first to make people dance, not for themselves only.

SB: What makes a good DJ?

QM: A DJ who can gather several assets: being different, technical, creative, generous, and most of all humble.

►John O'Callaghan

Ireland is known for many things: Guinness, shamrocks, and now John O'Callaghan. Firmly established in the A-list trance elite, John O'Callaghan is set to continue his journey further up the ladder of electronic dance superstardom. John's high-energy trance mix coupled with a highly refined precision mixing style has seen him surge up through the DJ ranks.

Spinning his first Radio 1 Essential Mix in the summer of 2008, the gifted twenty-nine-year-old was one of only four trance DJs to do so during the year. Immediately following that, he made his debut in *DJ Magazine*'s Top 100 DJs rundown, arriving at No. 60. In the 2009 chart, he became one of the year's highest climbers, leaping 36 places into the world's Top 25 (at number 24) and cemented his place as Ireland's foremost DJ and producer. In 2010 he held his own and remained in the Top 40 at No. 33, in a year where house music exploded into the poll–this was a great achievement to maintain his rank. In his home country he has picked up the Best DJ awards at the Irish Dance Music Awards for three consecutive years, decisively conquered the notoriously competitive testing ground of Ibiza, and was the first Irishman to play Trance Energy. John has achieved so much already, but this is just the beginning of a trance legacy.

SB: What inspired you to become a DJ?

J O'C: As a teenager I started going clubbing in Dublin in the Temple Theatre, where I seen DJs like Mauro Picotto and Timo Maas regularly. Mauro had a lot of charisma and I often thought I'd like to try it, but never thought I would.

SB: What are the three things you think most contributed to your success?

J O'C: I think consistency has been key for me; I try to produce high-quality trance on a regular basis, something that is not easy. The other thing would be location; Ireland is an easy country to travel to and from, so I can fly to any gig easily. The last would be luck, the aul rub of the green.

SB: What DJ'ing/mixing tip can you provide for readers that will help them become better DJs?

J O'C: To build sets that

take you on a journey, not just a bunch of music . . . listen to your music and love your music and play it with a creative mind.

SB: What makes a good DJ?
J O'C: A person who knows what record to play at the right time, to treat the crowd with respect and make the night enjoyable. Not to play hard music too early and to know when to peak, deliver that moment. Nice!

►DJ Heather

Brooklyn-born, Chicago-raised DJ Heather has been named one of Chicago's Top 45 Artists alongside Kanye West, Billy Corgan, and Green Velvet!

In the past few years, the Chicago house community has produced a number of innovative and distinct DJs trained in the art of transforming tranquil dance floors into spaces of sheer bedlam and bliss. Their committed vision of undiluted musical appreciation, interactive communication, improvisation, and basic integrity has brought greater attention to all the city's great DJs including the genre busting DJ Heather. Widely regarded as one of the premier selectors in the nation, this Chicagoan demonstrates her skills and sharp deck acumen for the massives throughout the Windy City and the world at large with verve and undeniable talent.

In 2006, DJ Heather toured extensively with Colette in support of their House of OM double-disc release. Following worldwide accolades, in 2007 Om Records announced *Summer Sessions 2*, mixed by Om family members DJ Heather and Onionz. The release followed the success of the first volume of the series mixed by Groove Junkies, Chuck Love, and DJ Fluid. In 2008 she joined fellow OM label artists—Colette, Fred Everything, and Andy Caldwell—on the House of OM Tour.

With over twenty years of experience behind her, DJ Heather has grown to become one of the Windy City's main DJ exports. She is an artist who defies conformity, defines quality and continues to nurture her solid skills for soul music of the technological generation.

SB: What inspired you to become a DJ?
DJ Heather: I'm a music nerdist who wanted to share their favorite things.

SB: What are the three things you think most contributed to your success?

DJ Heather: Dedication, practice, and being ready when opportunities presented themselves.

SB: What DJ'ing/mixing tip can you provide for readers that will help them become better DJs?

DJ Heather: Always adjust volumes in your headphones and monitors.

SB: What makes a good DJ?

DJ Heather: Remembering it's not always about you.

▶Re.You

It's been a steady climb for Marius Maier, better known as Re.You. His success in the electronic music scene, shifted from dreams into reality. Now firmly Berlin based, his prolific release schedule continues unabated, the live show with Rampa going from strength to strength as well as DJ sets at clubs across the world.

As a teenager in Ulm, a small town in southern Germany, Marius first began to appreciate the dark arts of beats through a love of DJ Premier's dark and jazzy cuts. Friends started all getting into turntablism but there were other things on his mind, especially after winning the German Youth Championship in basketball. A brutal knee injury ended these chances, but with a lot of spare recovery time on his hands, he began to teach himself production. Having fallen in with the Keinemusik crew around 2009, he soon developed a solid live partnership with Rampa. He describes their first night at Horst as one of the key moments in his career, and having previously only performed live, decided to devote himself to Re.You and start DJ'ing.

PHOTO BY MORITZ FUCHS

After destroying Room One Fabric with a Souvenir takeover, things heated up and Marius scored a massive hit with his edit of Lana Del Rey's"Video Games," which racked up about 50,000 listens in a week. The year 2012 has been extremely busy, with a hit on Mobilee called "Junction," "Yeah Yeah Yeah" on Cocoon, and a follow-up on Souvenir called "Falling," with haunting vocals supplied by fellow compatriot Daniel Wilde. His brother's new label, Avotre, has also recently played home to Fever, and with plenty more strings left to his bow, he has more singles scheduled to come out this year. It may be basketball's loss, but music fans across the world can rejoice at the inopportune accident that created this rising star. And better still, there's plenty more to come!

SB: What inspired you to become a DJ?
RY: I was playing basketball on a high level, practicing daily, [playing] games and [going to] training camp on the weekends. All quite successful. After a serious knee injury I suddenly had plenty of time for other things, so I started to experiment with some sounds and created my first tracks together with my brother Mathias.

SB: What are the three things you think most contributed to your success?

RY: That's a tough question. I think it's the hard work. I'm focusing on my music and keep working all the time. Another thing is the social part; I always try to have good relationships with others. If you do what you love, it's easy to show it. I think your soft skills are very important to have good success.

SB: What DJ'ing/mixing tip can you provide for readers that will help them become better DJs?

RY: You have to feel the music you play. It makes no sense to copy styles or sets. Just be yourself and try to enjoy what you do. Show your audience that you're happy and give them a good feeling. You can take them with you on your journey if you enjoy yourself.

SB: What makes a good DJ?

RY: The selection of tracks is very significant. A good DJ creates an amazing atmosphere if he can "read" the audience. Sometimes you need to push it forward; sometimes you should slow it down. For sure mixing skills are essential, as well as soft skills as I mentioned before.

►DJ Colette

Hers is a dedication that has driven Colette's career for more than fifteen years and counting. Never one to chase perpetually fleeting trends of dance music, her love and devotion to the authentic house sound of hometown Chicago has never flagged, and generations of die-hard fans never fail to appreciate it.

A pioneer in combining live vocals with her DJ set, Colette's singular sound still continues to evolve. Over two highly successful full-length artist albums—*Hypnotized* (2005) and *Push* (2007)—for legendary San Francisco imprint Om Records, she's shown the panoramic range of her musical influences. Shades of soul, jazz, and funk found on Colette's full-length recordings reveal an artist open to infinite possibilities.

Far from anonymous dance beats, original tracks like "What Will She Do for Love?" and "Feelin' Hypnotized" have become instantly recognizable signature songs and enduring fan favorites. "If" has the distinction of hitting No. 5 on *Billboard*'s Dance Club Play Chart. It's a sophisticated mix that's been a perfect fit for big-budget Hollywood soundtracks like *Sex and the City* and *The Devil Wears Prada*, both of which featured Colette's music prominently.

Famous for her jazzy alto voice, Colette has also been well documented for her exemplary DJ skills. With the release of her first mix CD, *In the Sun*, on underground Chicago label After Hours in 1999, Colette's tireless work ethic and crowd-pleasing sets culminated in her winning the Breakthrough DJ Award at the 2003 US Dancestar Awards in Miami.

A restless spirit always seeking new ways to share her love of genuine house music, Colette cohosted the nationally syndicated radio show *Maximum Rotation*. She and on-air partner Kevin Dees produced the show from the highly influential KIIS-FM radio station in Los Angeles from 2001 through 2004.

That same spirit has led to Colette's latest achievement: successfully launching the fledgling Candy Talk record label, a goal Colette has had for the better part of a decade.

"It's something I've always wanted to do. It's a lot like why I started DJ'ing. It allows me to have more creative control," she enthuses about her imprint. "I only work with producers I genuinely like. Whomever I'm playing the most in my DJ sets, that's the person I seek out to work with on Candy Talk," she says passionately. "It's just another aspect of the industry for me to learn."

SB: What inspired you to become a DJ?

DJ Colette: Growing up in Chicago I was introduced to house music at a very young age. I also studied classical voice for most of my childhood. At the age of sixteen I met DJ Lego, and he invited me to sing over some of his sets. I was instantly hooked. I figured if I learned how to DJ I'd be able to sing all the time. I acquired a pair of turntables from DJ Sneak and spent most of the next year figuring out how to play records. In 1997 I played my first set at the debut of Superjane.

SB: What are the three things you think most contributed to your success?

DJ Colette: [The first is that] music is intoxicating to me. It's been my passion since I was a little girl and something that I always wanted to be a part of. [Second,] I work at my craft all the time. I rarely take days off. I'm just as interested in the business side of things as I am the artistic. [Third,] I try not to follow trends. I'm very honest about the music that I make. I don't classify myself as underground or commercial. I just try to make music that moves me . . . and hopefully moves you, too.

SB: What DJ'ing/mixing tip can you provide for readers that will help them become better DJs?

DJ Colette: Remember that mixing on beat is just as important as bringing the next track in at the correct measure. It's the most basic skill, but it lays down the foundation for you to become a master technician. I recently witnessed a few DJs who ignored this, and although their mixes were on beat, the two songs couldn't be blended together for more than a moment. There was no harmony between them. It was actually more offensive than "shoes in the dryer."

SB: What makes a good DJ?

DJ Colette: A good DJ always has that "wow" moment that takes you by surprise. It may be a particular track that gets ya or a specific mix, but it's a moment that you won't forget. You'll probably tell stories about it later, [like] "Remember when they played that record? That shit was crazyyy!" That's what makes a good DJ.

▶Gramophonedzie

Marko Milićević is Gramophonedzie, the MTV award-winning Serbian superstar who is currently riding a serious wave following a remarkable breakthrough year back in 2010. From his hometown of Belgrade, he has forged a loyal worldwide following for his distinctive productions and performances.

With his roots spanning a wide musical spectrum and a deep passion for funky music, live instruments and intensive vocals, his production career began in 2000 when he was selected to study at the Red Bull Music Academy in Ireland. He subsequently completed a degree in Sound Design at Belgrade University and went on to produce soundtracks for a number of commercials, films, and television as well as producing for several Serbian bands.

Gramophonedzie has been voted Best Adria Act during the 2010 MTV European Music Awards and was additionally nominated in the Best European Act category alongside artists such as Enrique Inglesias, Swedish House Mafia, and Marina & the Diamonds. As a DJ, Marko tours internationally and has a dedicated dance floor congregation across the globe. In the past twelve months, he has toured extensively throughout Europe as well as played across Australia, Brazil, Hong Kong, and the United States, and rocked dance floors in destinations such as Dubai, Russia, and Indonesia. With his proven record, a full touring schedule, and a host of new productions ready to drop, 2012 looks set to be another big year for Gramophonedzie.

SB: What inspired you to become a DJ?
MM: I was twelve or thirteen and went to the UK to improve my English language, while one day wandering around London—I think Camden—I stumbled across some shop with clothes and in the basement there was a record shop and they were playing jungle at that moment. Decks spinning . . . I dunno what happened there, but like I got under some spell that kept me till today. There is definitely something magical and hypnotic in watching 1210 decks spin.

SB: What are the three things you think most contributed to your success?

MM: DJ'ing is my life, and persistence to keep doing what I love brought me to my success and living my dream; second is hard work; and third is big support from my parents, friends, and lately, my wife, who stands behind every decision I make.

SB: What DJ'ing/mixing tip can you provide for readers that will help them become better DJs?

MM: Listen to all kinds of music—everything, but I mean everything—and play as many different parties that you can—from weddings to birthdays, café's, clubs, festivals—and also try to play as many genres as you can. That will make you gain experience, which is most important for DJs, and make you capable of reading every crowd you stumble across in your future career.

SB: What makes a good DJ?

MM: A DJ that can entertain any crowd with his music selection only. A DJ who will make people dance and enjoy the music he plays even if they don't like it in the first place. That's a great DJ, one who discovers new galaxies in someone's music universe.

musicPRO guides

Quality Instruction, Professional Results

Prices, contents, and availability subject to change without notice.

Hal Leonard Books
An Imprint of Hal Leonard Corporation
www.musicproguides.com